SPECIAL
The Science

Contents

Parts of this edition were previously published by TIME, Health *and* Real Simple.

The Incredible Medicine of Movement

People have more power than they think to shape their own health destinies. The secret is exercise

BY DR. JORDAN D. METZL

EXERCISE IS A MIRACLE DRUG. I'M SUCH A BELIEVER THAT it's the key to health, wellness and longevity that I prescribe it to every patient I see.

Take it often, and you'll live a longer, healthier life. Your medical costs will be lower, you'll sleep better at night, and your workdays will be more productive. Your mood will improve, and your risk of developing almost any chronic disease will drop.

It works for just about everyone who takes it, young or old, and if done correctly, it has few or no negative side effects. Every dose is 100% effective—even small ones. It's the most powerful, readily available drug in the world. And it's free.

As a sports medicine physician at the Hospital for Special Surgery in New York, plus an athlete and fitness instructor, I know how far the field of medicine is from embracing this prescription. Health care in the United States is, in practice, more like "sick care." We spend much more money treating an increasingly unhealthy population years down the line, after disease has set in, instead of investing in preventive ways to avoid it in the first place.

But over the past 60 years, scientific research has provided irrefutable evidence of the medicinal value of exercise. For the country to reduce health-care costs and enhance well-being, the worlds of fitness and medi-

Jordan Metzl, a sports medicine physician, teaches free fitness classes in New York—like this one, at the Intrepid Sea, Air and Space Museum.

cine must come closer together and put this precious medicine to good use.

IT'S ARMOR FOR THE BODY

The powerful medicine of exercise does more than just make you feel better after a jog or spin class. It works across the entire body to help shield it from disease.

Modern medicine got a taste of this potential in 1953, when a study published in the scientific journal *The Lancet* showed that British postmen tended to die less from heart attacks and heart failure than people like mail sorters, who were employed in more sedentary jobs. Early studies like these established the link between activity and disease prevention and inspired further research.

We now have proof that several diseases respond strongly to exercise. Active people have lower blood pressure, stroke rates and heart-attack risk than those who do not exercise regularly, suggesting that exercise is a powerful foe against heart disease, the number-one killer in the U.S. It even affects a person's risk for cancer. A 2016 study of more than 1.4 million people showed regular exercise decreases the risk for 13 types of cancer, including breast, ovarian and colon cancer. Type 2 diabetes—which costs hundreds of billions of dollars per year and affects nearly 30 million Americans—is both preventable and treatable with regular exercise.

The known benefits of exercise even apply to the brain. Numerous studies have shown lower rates of anxiety, depression and memory loss among regular exercisers, compared with people who don't move around much. Exercise is currently the most effective known way to prevent the much-feared conditions of dementia and Alzheimer's disease and to slow their progression.

EVERYONE CAN EXERCISE

Thankfully, you don't need to take megadoses of this drug to get the benefits. A little bit goes a long way.

The American College of Sports Medicine recommends 150 minutes of exercise per week—just about 30 minutes, five days a week. More is better, but this seems to be the sweet spot. Anything from brisk walking to jogging to hightailing it up the stairs counts. And the harder you're willing to push yourself, the less time you'll have to commit to enduring it. You can get away with half of the recommended dose of exercise by exercising at high intensity, like in the popular workout of high-intensity interval training, or HIIT.

Nearly everyone can add more exercise into their lives—even people whose bodies have been through a lot. Five years ago, I started a full-body workout class, called IronStrength, in the basement of a local gym with 20 of my patients. I had found that the stronger I kept my own muscles, the fewer aches and pains I had in my hips and knees, so why not help my patients get those same results?

Today, IronStrength workouts have grown from 20 to 1,000 people, sometimes more. We now hold them in outdoor spaces like Central Park or on the flight deck of the Intrepid Sea, Air and Space Museum.

What started as a way to teach people to strengthen their muscles has turned into a program that attracts people of all ages, sizes and fitness levels. Regular attendees include

People of all ages can benefit from strength training. IronStrength classes have drawn people as young as 10 and as old as 71 to Central Park in the summer.

people like Cheryl, who ran her first half-marathon at age 62, and Ben, who was side-lined with a chronic hamstring injury until strength exercises helped him heal. In one recent class, a 10-year old, her 42-year-old mother and her 71-year-old grandmother were all doing the same exercises.

The success of these free, weekly classes proves that getting in shape doesn't have to be painful or expensive. When we surveyed participants last year, most said they kept coming back to class because doing it as a group made exercise social and fun. Exercise isn't just good for the body; it also has the power to engage and build communities.

A FITTER FUTURE

As movements like these spread across the country, and as mainstream medicine slowly starts to catch up with the research, the hope is that physicians and health insurers can work together to educate patients about preventive health and find ways to incentivize exercise.

If I had my way, medicine's four core vital signs—temperature, pulse, blood pressure and respiration rate—would be joined by a fifth: step count, with a goal of 10,000 per day. It should be part of every standard medical chart, right alongside height and weight.

We must embrace exercise as preventive medicine, because what we're doing now isn't working. Every year, Americans spend more than $3 trillion on health care, and most of that goes toward treating diseases. Ours is by far the most expensive in the world, yet Americans aren't especially healthy. With an average life expectancy of 78.8 years, the U.S. ranks 43rd among all nations in longevity and population health. For both doctors and patients, embracing exercise is the key to driving these costs down and improving people's outcomes.

Eventually, exercise will be prescribed as a real medicine, down to the dosage. Patients will be incentivized to exercise in ways specifically designed for them, based on their age, fitness level and interests. They'll be able to join virtual group classes and participate together, creating digital communities. All of these programs would encourage people to move more.

There's no need to wait for health-care reform to validate what science has already shown to be true: that exercise is a potent preventive medicine, far safer and more effective than any other drug on the market. Though plenty of people love it, it's a tougher sell for those who don't. Yes, taking a pill to lower cholesterol or blood pressure is easier than going for a run to meet the same goal. But remember—if a drug was invented that had all the benefits of exercise, people would fight to get their hands on it.

As today's medical world advances at a dizzying rate, it's equally important to get back to basics. Whatever your age and wherever you live, maximize your own dose of exercise: get moving, keep moving, and don't stop.

Jordan D. Metzl is a renowned sports-medicine physician at the Hospital for Special Surgery in New York. In addition to his medical practice, he has written five books, including *Dr. Jordan Metzl's Workout Prescription* (2016), and created the IronStrength Workout and IronStrength community fitness program to promote activity and wellness.

PART ONE

why to work out

How exercise wards off disease, sharpens your brain and keeps you in your prime for longer

The New Science of Exercise

Doctors, researchers, scientists and even ancient philosophers have long claimed that exercise works like a miracle drug. Now they have proof

BY MANDY OAKLANDER

EVER SINCE HIGH SCHOOL, MARK Tarnopolsky has blurred the line between jock and nerd. After working out every morning and doing 200 push-ups, he runs three miles to his lab at McMaster University in Ontario. When he was younger, Tarnopolsky dreamed of becoming a gym teacher. But now, in his backup career as a genetic metabolic neurologist, he's determined to prove that exercise can be used as medicine for even the sickest patients.

"People would always say to me, 'Exercise? Come on. Scientifically, you can't come up with a mechanism, so it's a complete waste of time,' " Tarnopolsky says. "But as time goes on, paper after paper after paper shows that the most effective, potent way that we can improve quality of life and duration of life is exercise."

Tarnopolsky has published some of those papers himself. In 2011, he and a team studied mice with a terrible genetic disease that caused them to age prematurely. Over the course of five months, half of the mice were sedentary. The other half were coaxed to run three times a week on a miniature treadmill.

By the end of the study, the sedentary mice were barely hanging on. The fur that had yet to fall out had grown coarse and gray, muscles shriveled, hearts weakened, skin thinned—even the mice's hearing got worse. "They were shivering in the corner, about to die," Tarnopolsky says.

But the group of mice that exercised, genetically compromised though they were, were nearly indistinguishable from healthy mice. Their coats were sleek and black, they ran around their cages, they could even reproduce. "We almost completely prevented the premature aging in the animals," Tarnopolsky says.

That's remarkable news, if you're a mouse. And though there are obvious differences between rodents and humans, Tarnopolsky has seen something similar happen in his ill patients. "I've seen all the hype about gene therapy for people with genetic disease"—Tarnopolsky treats kids with severe genetic diseases like muscular dystrophy—"but it hasn't delivered in the 25 years I've been doing this," he says. "The most effective therapy available to my patients right now is exercise."

Tarnopolsky now thinks he knows why. In studies in which blood is drawn immediately after people exercised, researchers have found that many positive changes occur throughout the body during and right after a workout. "Going for a run is going to improve your skin health, your eye health, your gonadal health," he says. "It's unbelievable." If there were a drug that could do for human health everything that exercise can, it would likely be the most valuable pharmaceutical ever developed.

The trouble is that only 20% of Americans get the recommended 150 minutes of strength and cardiovascular physical activity per week, more than half of all baby boomers report doing no exercise whatsoever, and 80.2 million Americans over age 6 are entirely inactive.

Humans are notoriously bad at assessing the long-term benefits—and risks—of their lifestyle choices.

The consequences of a sedentary life are as well documented as they are dire. People with low levels of physical activity are at a higher risk for many different kinds of cancer, heart disease, Alzheimer's disease and early death by any cause. That's at the end of life. Long before that, inactivity can worsen arthritis symptoms, increase lower-back pain, and lead to depression and anxiety, not to mention cause a sallow complexion.

Despite public-awareness campaigns, the health benefits of exercise have not been effectively communicated to the average American. Humans are notoriously bad at assessing the long-term benefits—and risks—of their lifestyle choices. And vague promises that exercise is "good for you" or even "good for the heart" aren't powerful enough to motivate most people to do something they think of as a chore. Humans are, however, motivated by rewards. That is why experts like Tarnopolsky are so focused on proving that the scientific benefits of exercise—slower aging, better mood, less chronic pain, stronger vision, the list goes on—are real, measurable and almost immediate.

EXERCISE BASICS, EXPLAINED

Incorporating exercise into your week doesn't have to be complicated. Here are some common exercise questions answered:

HOW MUCH EXERCISE DO I REALLY NEED TO BE DOING?

The World Health Organization and the U.S. Centers for Disease Control and Prevention advise most adults to do 150 minutes of moderate-intensity aerobic physical activity each week and twice-weekly muscle strengthening.

WHAT COUNTS AS MODERATE-INTENSITY EXERCISE?

Everything you think of as exercise—plus lots of stuff you don't, including brisk walking, playing with the kids, walking the dog, carrying heavy groceries and gardening. Do at least 10 minutes at a time, and break it up however you want.

IS HIGH-INTENSITY INTERVAL TRAINING AS GOOD AS REGULAR EXERCISE?

More research is needed, but evidence suggests that short, all-out bursts of exercise bring unique benefits. They're also a great option for the time-crunched. New research shows that as long as you go hard, intervals are just as effective as longer workouts, even for some people with chronic diseases.

I HATE LIFTING WEIGHTS. CAN I JUST DO CARDIO?

Sorry, but if your goal is to live longer and healthier, you should do both, because they offer different benefits. Cardio will prevent you from being winded after climbing stairs, while strength training will build muscle and bone, which protects against injury.

The National Institutes of Health (NIH) is on the bandwagon too. This year the agency is launching a massive study with the aim of documenting in unprecedented detail exactly what happens inside a body in motion. Its hope: to prove that exercise is medicine.

Before doctors adopted a single-minded focus on treating and curing diseases, their main goal was to keep people healthy. Even back in 400 B.C., doctors knew that diet and exercise were the best ways to do that. "Eating alone will not keep a man well," Hippocrates famously wrote. "He must also take exercise." For millennia, doctors were the vanguards of physical education, the original PE teachers.

But in the early 1900s, with the rise of modern surgery and nascent pharmaceuticals, medicine shifted its focus from the prevention of disease to its treatment. Paradoxically, physicians de-emphasized exercise just as the modern Olympics swelled in popularity and colleges began building campus stadiums to accommodate America's growing love of spectator sports. The authors of a paper published in a 1905 issue of the *Journal of the American Medical Association* mourned how many people were losing sight of the health benefits of exercise. "The men on the teams are the very ones whom Nature has endowed superabundantly with physical capacity, but on them the physical director bends most of his energies," they wrote, "while the average student is left to get his physical development by yelling from the bleachers."

Physical activity was no longer the medicine of the masses but the privilege of elite athletes. When scientists studied exercise, it was to figure out how athletes could improve their peak performance, not how mere mortals could improve their health day to day. This gap persists. At a time when boutique (read: expensive) fitness studios are more popular than ever, fewer people are getting the minimum recommended amount of exercise.

Worse, many U.S. schools have seen gym classes cut from the curriculum; nearly half of high school students don't have a weekly PE class, and only 15% of elementary schools require PE at least three days a week for the school year. The result: the majority of American kids and adolescents have so-called

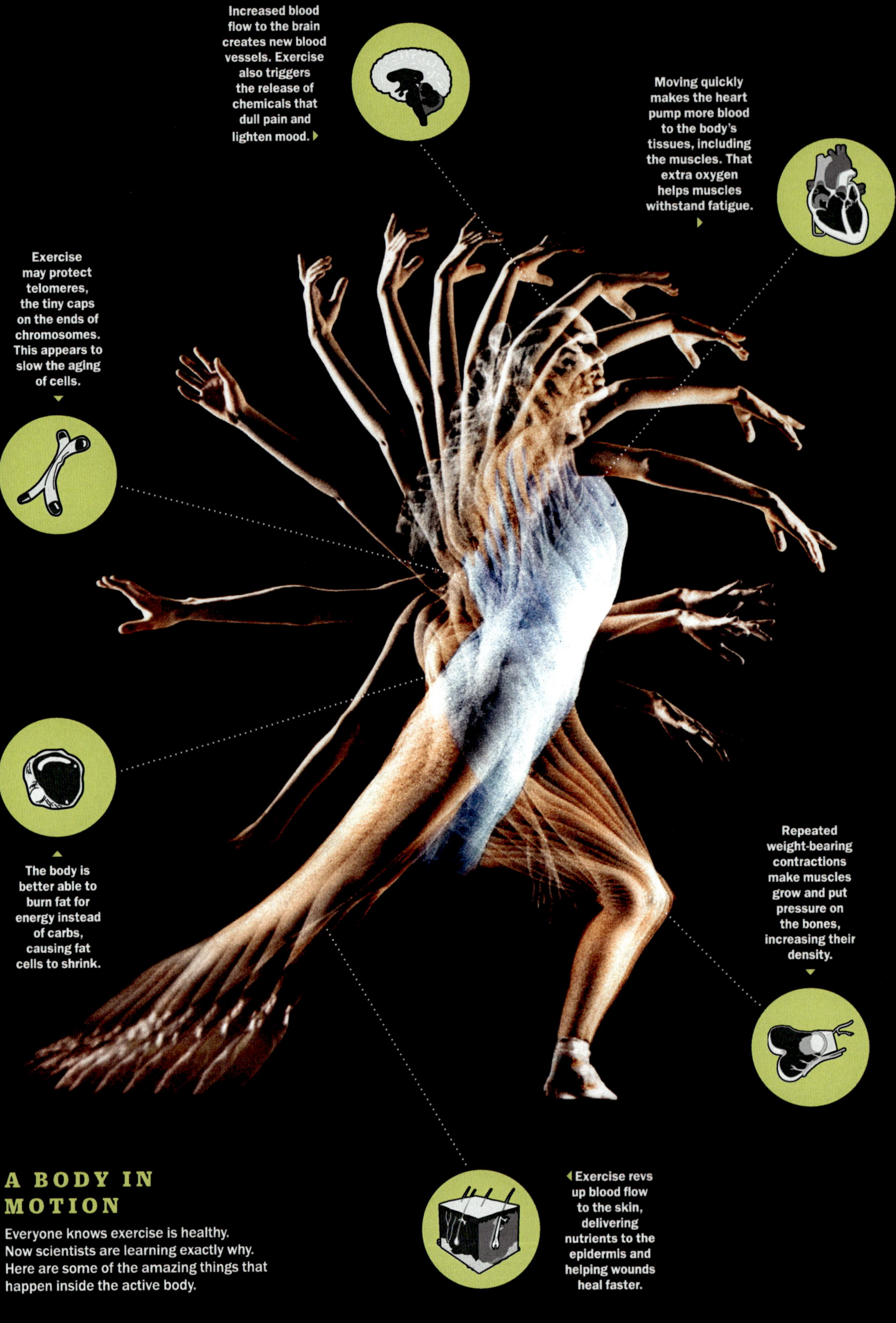

A BODY IN MOTION

Everyone knows exercise is healthy. Now scientists are learning exactly why. Here are some of the amazing things that happen inside the active body.

exercise-deficit disorder. Meanwhile, childhood obesity rates have climbed every year since 1999. "You have whole generations that are soured on exercise," says Jack Berryman, a professor emeritus of medical history at the University of Washington School of Medicine.

Researchers like Tarnopolsky and Marcas Bamman, an exercise physiologist who is part of the NIH study, are hoping that their work will begin reversing those trends. Next year the NIH will launch its six-year, $170 million study with a group of about 3,000 sedentary people, ranging from children to the elderly. The subjects will start an exercise program and then submit blood, fat and muscle samples before and after they exercise. Scientists will then examine the samples for clues to how the body changes with physical activity. A control group that doesn't exercise will also be tracked for comparison.

Recent research links exercise to less depression, better memory and quicker learning.

As part of the study, researchers will do the same experiment in animals to get tissue samples from places like the brain and the lungs that would be too dangerous to obtain from humans. "It'll be a tremendously enormous data set," says Maren Laughlin, the program director for integrative metabolism at the NIH, who is also a lead researcher on the new study. In the end, the researchers think, they'll be able to identify every single molecule in the body that's tweaked or turned on by exercise.

This kind of study—its size, its rigor, its aims—is a first, and experts are hoping it will give doctors the evidence they need to start treating exercise like the miracle drug they've long thought it to be. "If you think of exercise as a true form of medicine, which it is, it's not good enough to just look at a patient and say, 'You need to do more exercise,' " says Bamman, director of the Center for Exercise Medicine at the University of Alabama at Birmingham. "That's no better than handing someone a bottle of pills and saying, 'Here, take a few,' " with no other explanation.

Bamman is betting that with this new data, exercise will one day be prescribed to patients. Instead of leaving the doctor's office with nothing but a slip of paper with a drug name scrawled on it, patients may also get a detailed exercise plan tailored to make their medication work better. "We think that precision will go a long way in changing behavior," Bamman says. "We're at a really important time in the field."

Think of all the different ways you can sweat, and you might be surprised that each falls into one of just two categories. You're doing aerobic exercise when your breathing speeds up, your blood flows faster and your heart pumps more of it, shooting oxygen out to the tissues in the rest of the body. It's the most popular kind; about half of Americans meet the recommendations for aerobic physical activity. But only 20% also do the other type, strength training. The phrase may conjure grunting weight lifters and gym dumbbells slick with sweat, but to build muscle and strengthen bones, you really only need to use your body weight as resistance, says Anthony Hackney, an exercise physiologist at the University of North Carolina. That's why things like yoga, tai chi and Pilates—not just pumping iron—are excellent forms of strength training. "People always get the image of the big, muscular guy," Hackney says. "We try to think of muscle strength and power as a 65-year-old lady picking up a gallon of milk, pouring a glass and feeling comfortable."

In addition to the heart, muscles, lungs and bones, scientists are finding that another major beneficiary of exercise might be the brain. Recent research links exercise to less depression, better memory and quicker learning. Studies also suggest that exercise is, as of now, the best way to prevent or delay the onset of Alzheimer's, which is second only to cancer as the disease Americans fear most, according to surveys.

Scientists don't know exactly why exercise changes the structure and function of the brain for the better, but it's an area of active research. So far, they've found that exercise improves blood flow to the brain, feeding the growth of new blood vessels and even new brain cells, courtesy of the protein BDNF, short for brain-derived neurotrophic factor. BDNF triggers the growth of new neurons and helps repair and protect brain cells from degeneration. "I always tell people that exercise is regenerative medicine—restoring and repairing and basically fixing things that are broken," Bamman says.

Repairs like this throughout the body may be the reason exercise has been shown to extend life span by as much as five years. A small new study suggests that moderate-intensity exercise may slow down the aging of cells. As humans get older and their cells divide over and over again, their telomeres—the protective caps on the end of chromosomes—get shorter. To see how exercise affects telomeres, researchers took muscle biopsies and blood samples from 10 healthy people before and after a 45-minute ride on a stationary bicycle. They found that exercise increased levels of a molecule that protects telomeres, ultimately slowing how quickly they shorten over time. Exercise, then, appears to slow aging at the cellular level.

Exercise has been shown to extend life span by as much as five years.

For all its merits, however, exercise is not an effective way to lose weight, research has shown. In a cruel twist, many people actually gain weight after they start exercising, whether from new muscle mass or a fired-up appetite. "Some people say exercise doesn't do anything," says researcher John Jakicic of the University of Pittsburgh. "Well, exercise does a lot. It just may not show up on the scale."

One of the best pieces of news is that so much of what we already do counts as physical activity. "Mowing the grass, raking leaves, washing the car—all that's exercise," says Berryman, the exercise historian. "Physical activity includes all movement, not just throwing a ball through a basket."

What's more, emerging research suggests that it doesn't take much movement to get the benefits. "We've been interested in the question of, How low can you go?" says Martin Gibala, an exercise physiologist at McMaster University. After all, if it were possible to reap all the health benefits of exercise in a tiny fraction of the time, who wouldn't be compelled to give it a try?

Gibala wanted to test how efficient and effective a 10-minute workout could be, compared with the standard 50-minutes-at-a-time approach. The micro-workout he devised consists of three exhausting 20-second bouts of all-out, hard-as-you-can exercise, followed by brief recoveries. In a three-month study, he pitted the short workout against the standard one to see which was better.

To his amazement, the workouts resulted in identical improvements in heart function and blood-sugar control, even though one workout was five times as long as the other. "If you're willing and able to push hard, you can get away with surprisingly little exercise," Gibala says.

Not everyone can—or wants to—do this kind of excruciating workout, often referred to as high-intensity interval training, or HIIT. Many of us would gladly bounce around in Zumba class for an hour to avoid enduring even a minute of HIIT torture. But considering that a lack of time is the No. 1 reason people say they don't exercise, a workout that's far shorter than what's generally recommended could be a strong motivator. Gibala, for his part, is wondering if the workout can get even shorter. He's even played around with the idea of a one-minute workout.

Not every type of exercise will work for every person, of course, but a growing body of research indicates that very vigorous exercise—like the interval workouts Gibala is studying—is, in fact, appropriate for people with different chronic conditions, from Type 2 diabetes to heart failure. That's new thinking, because for decades, people with certain diseases and even pregnant women were advised not to exercise. Now scientists know that far more people can and should exercise. A recent analysis of more than 300 clinical trials discovered that for people recovering from a stroke, for instance, exercise was even more effective at helping them rehabilitate.

Robert Sallis, a family physician who runs a sports-medicine fellowship at Kaiser Permanente Fontana Medical Center in California, has prescribed exercise to his patients

Minor daily moves—not just throwing a ball through a basket—can count as exercise.

since the early 1990s in hopes of doling out less medication. "It really worked amazingly, particularly in my very sickest patients," he says. "If I could get them to do it on a regular basis—even just walking, anything that got their heart rate up a bit—I would see dramatic improvements in their chronic disease, not to mention all of these other things like depression, anxiety, mood and energy levels."

Older people, too, can benefit from strenuous exercise. Until now, all the recommendations for increasing bone density have included low-repetition, high-weight types of training, says Jinger Gottschall, an associate professor of kinesiology at Penn State University. "But this just isn't feasible for a lot of people. You can't picture your grandma going in and doing that." Luckily for Grandma, Gottschall's team found that lifting lighter weights for more reps improves bone density in key parts of the body, making it a good alternative to heavy lifting.

It's becoming evident that nearly everyone—young, old, pregnant, ill—benefits from exercise. And as scientists learn more about why that is, they're hoping that those early-20th-century missteps—the move away from our being bodies in motion—will be reversed. They're also hoping that the messaging around exercise gets simpler. "People think now, because of the health-club and fitness movement, that in order to exercise you need to join a fancy club and wear fancy clothes," says Berryman. In fact, some of the best exercise, research is showing, doesn't require a gym membership at all.

Back at McMaster University, Tarnopolsky and his team are almost finished doing autopsies on mice from their new study, and even though the scalpel-wielding scientists are blind to which groups the mice were in, they can tell with certainty which animals were allowed to exercise and which were sedentary. "You open up the sedentary mice, and there's fat all over the place," he says. About half of those mice have tumors. "They just look god-awful." As for the mice who hit the wheel every day? "We haven't found a single tumor," he says. "I think if people saw, they'd be pretty motivated to exercise."

The Fitness Rx

Is your DNA your destiny? Not if you exercise, suggests new research. Here's what kind of workout will work the best (and do the most for you)

BY CAMILLE NOE PAGÁN

YOU ALREADY KNOW THAT PHYSICAL ACTIVITY IS GOOD FOR you. What you may not realize is just how much of a game changer it can be. In a recent study published in the journal *Medicine & Science in Sports & Exercise*, researchers looked at 10 pairs of male identical twins in their 30s. Each twin was similar to his brother in most ways, right down to their eating habits—except that one in each pair had stopped exercising regularly in adulthood. Despite the fact that the less active twins had the exact same DNA as their fit brothers, after just three sedentary years, they had begun to develop insulin resistance (a precursor to diabetes), had more body fat and lower endurance—and, perhaps most notably, had less gray matter in the brain regions responsible for motor control and coordination. While the study was small, it's evidence that exercise may have as large an effect on your health as your genes do.

Of course, when you're debating whether to respond to two dozen unopened emails or go for a jog, "good health" can become an abstract concept to be worried about on another day. A simple way to make exercise more pressing—and desirable—is to take a goal-oriented approach. Research shows that certain forms of physical activity are particularly effective for specific objectives, and getting results will motivate you to lace up your gym shoes again and again. Here's how to match your workout to your needs and tap into the power of movement.

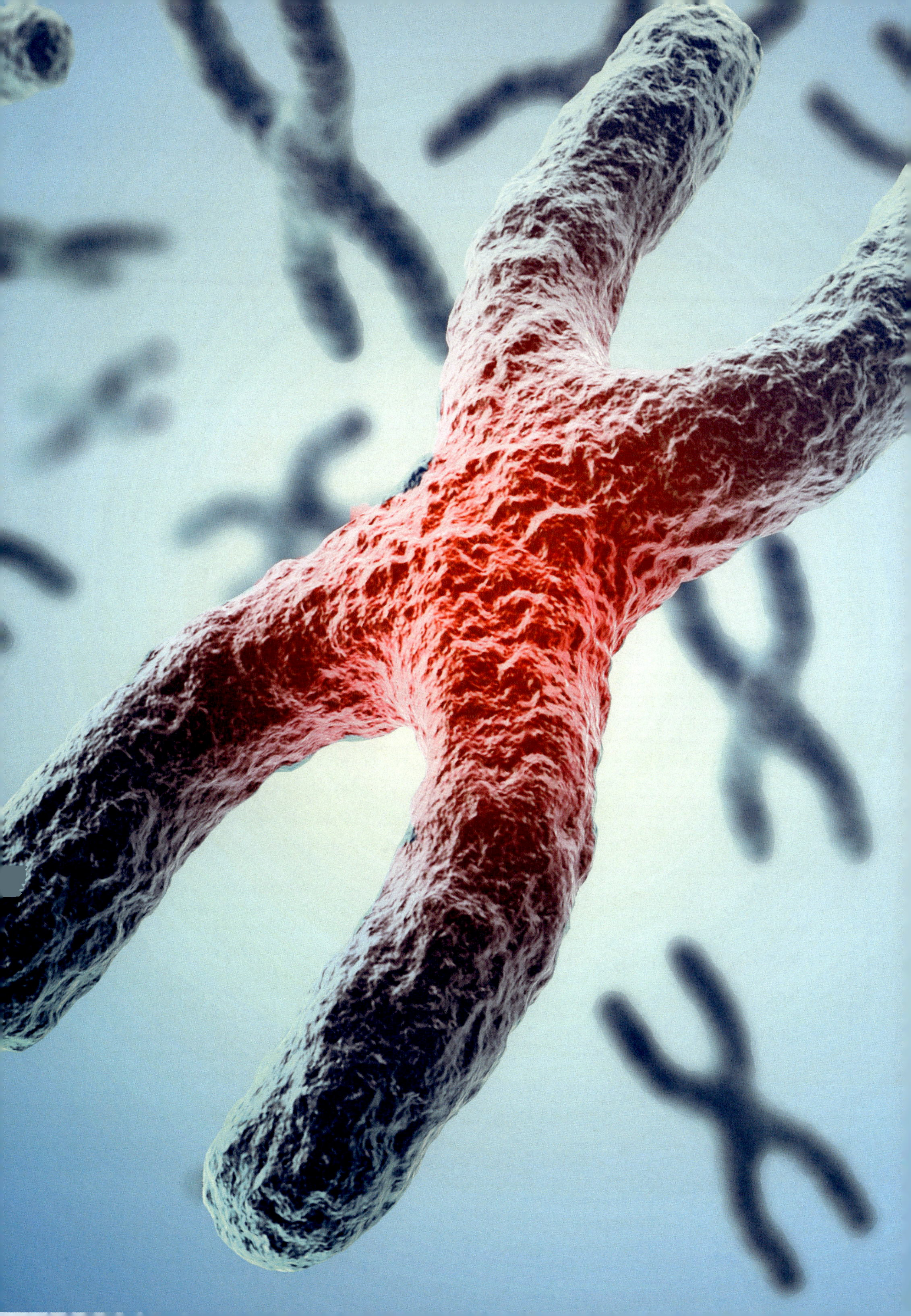

If you want more energy... do any kind of exercise three to four times a week

Regular exercise increases energy and reduces fatigue in adults of all ages with various health conditions—even the kinds that cause exhaustion, like fibromyalgia—and in people who are healthy, too, according to a 2006 University of Georgia review of 70 studies. The study authors found that just 20 minutes of low- to moderate-intensity activity (including biking, walking, strength training and stretching) a few times a week improved energy in as little as four weeks. "Exercise evens out your fluid and salt balance, helps your body use sugar [in the bloodstream] and burns fat. Or as I often say, it helps you sweat out the mayonnaise," says Tim Church, a professor at Louisiana State University's Pennington Biomedical Research Center. "It fundamentally helps you feel better." What's more, "physical activity increases the size and number of your mitochondria, which are the cellular powerhouses that help your body operate efficiently," notes Stella Volpe, the chair of the department of nutrition sciences at Drexel University.

If you want to limit your doctor's visits... count your steps with a Fitbit

Sitting is the new smoking. Research shows that the less you move, the higher your risk of, well, just about every health problem. "A hundred years ago, Americans spent their waking hours doing physically demanding tasks," says Steven Blair, an exercise scientist and professor at the University of South Carolina. "Today the average person sits at work all day, then goes home and sits in front of the television." But you don't need to join CrossFit to undo the ill effects of an office job and live a longer, healthier life, says Blair. Instead, try to move more. Also, consider using a fitness-tracking device, like a Fitbit or a Garmin watch. The device will give you a reasonably accurate estimate of how active you are by logging your steps as you do activities like gardening, cleaning and taking bathroom breaks. Any number over zero is good, but "7,000 steps a day, and you're vastly improving your health," says Church.

And yes, all movement counts. According to a 2013 study published in *Preventive Medicine*, people who did short bursts of physical activity—for example, raking leaves or pacing while talking on the phone—for a total of 150 minutes a week were as healthy as people who logged similar amounts of aerobic exercise (like biking). They had similar blood pressure, cholesterol levels, waist circumference and level of C-reactive protein (an inflammatory marker found in the blood that is linked to health problems such as heart disease and arthritis).

If you want to ease a chronic health problem... see a pro and go slow

When you're dealing with an ongoing health issue, it may seem tempting—safer, even—to avoid exercise, but that's exactly the time you can most benefit from movement. Exercise eases the symptoms of many chronic conditions, such as arthritis. And in the case of high blood pressure and Type 2 diabetes, it can even reverse them. It also reduces pain by increasing blood flow and promoting the release of feel-good brain chemicals, like endorphins.

To avoid injury and burnout, begin slowly. "Start with 10 minutes, or even five, several times a week," advises Volpe. "You want to build strength and endurance over the course of several months." Get your doctor's OK before starting a new exercise program, but keep in mind that many physicians have little or no fitness expertise. A physical therapist or an American College of Sports Medicine–certified physiologist or personal trainer can help you create a personalized plan.

If you're trying to lose weight (or keep it off)... combine strength training and cardio

Exercise alone usually won't take the extra pounds off; you have to curb your calorie intake for that to happen. (That's why a study published this year in the *Journal of Strength and Conditioning Research* found that most sedentary women who did three weekly, high-intensity treadmill workouts for 12 weeks but didn't change their eating habits were not able to lose weight.) Data, however, from the National Weight Control Registry—an ongoing, decades-long study of people who lose a significant amount of weight—shows that those who maintain a large loss do so in part by exercising most days of the week.

"You should be doing a combination of aerobic exercise and strength training," says Cedric Bryant, the chief science officer of the American Council on Exercise. Aerobic exercise burns calories that would otherwise be stored as extra pounds. Strength training builds and preserves muscle mass, "which can offset age-related muscle loss, keeping your metabolism revved, even during menopause," says Bryant.

Aim for at least 150 minutes of moderate-intensity aerobic exercise a week. But if you do high-intensity workouts, like running or spinning, you can cut that amount in half. Do at least two weekly strength-training sessions, too, by lifting weights or doing Pilates, yoga or resistance exercises (think planks and push-ups).

If you want to be less stressed or depressed... exercise regularly—but not too hard

"The real reason to get excited about exercise is because it makes you feel great," says Bradley Cardinal, a co-director of the Sport and Exercise Psychology Lab at Oregon State University. Women who engage in regular physical activity tend to have less stress and anxiety and higher self-esteem than do those who are inactive, even during tough times.

If you are blue or have been diagnosed with depression, aerobic exercise is an especially effective mood booster. But "other forms of exercise, such as yoga and strength training, can help too," says Jeffrey Katula, an associate professor in the department of health and exercise science at Wake Forest University. Perhaps the best example is a now famous Duke University study published in 1999 that found that depressed adults who did 45 minutes of aerobic exercise three times a week improved their mood as much as did those who took the prescription antidepressant Zoloft instead of exercising.

"Exercise takes you out of your head; it's harder to worry when you're focusing on where you're walking or whether you can hit the tennis ball," says Teresa Gevedon, a psychiatrist at the University of Kentucky, who often prescribes exercise to patients with depression and anxiety. It also increases mood-boosting brain chemicals, such as serotonin and endorphins, which ease pain and increase pleasure while lowering levels of the stress hormone cortisol.

But steer clear of any form of exercise that feels difficult or uncomfortable while you're doing it (such as sprints or a punishing spinning class), advises Katula: "Though a negative experience during exercise is temporary, it may be enough to keep you from going back and doing it again." Even "light" exercise, like walking, will help you feel better, provided you do it most days. "When it comes to mood, the effects of exercise may only last about 24 hours," says Gevedon.

FITNESS THROUGHOUT THE AGES

Ancient push-up programs, the rise of frolicking, and 23 other milestones in exercise history

BY MERRILL FABRY

1500 B.C.—The Olmec civilization in Mexico develops a game in which players used their hips, bottom, knees and elbows to move a heavy rubber ball through a ring.

1400 B.C.—Pharaohs' tombs depict the kings' athletic prowess in running, wrestling and archery competitions.

776 B.C.—The Olympic Games begin, and gymnasiums prosper. Being fit is viewed as the duty of a nation to be ready for war.

1316—Jeu de paume, a type of handball popular among nobility and played against a wall, kills French King Louis X, according to lore.

14th–15th centuries—Mob or folk football is played in medieval Europe. Widely disparaged for its violence, it was routinely banned.

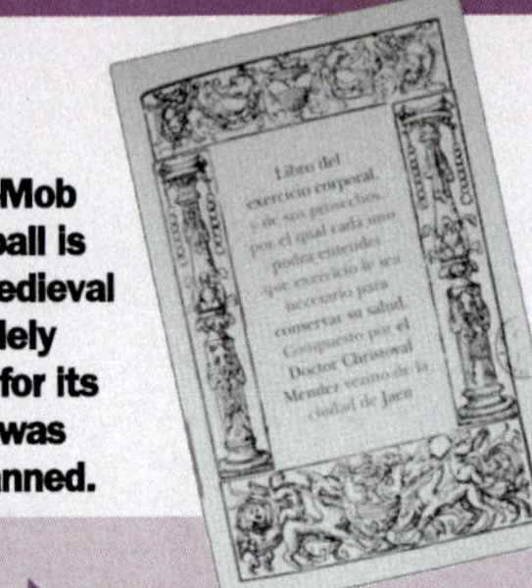

1553—The first exercise book is published by Spanish physician Cristobal Mendez. Walking is the most healthful kind, he claims.

1786—Thomas Jefferson extols the virtues of fitness, writing that "not less than two hours a day should be devoted to exercise, and the weather should be little regarded."

1824—Women are finally encouraged to do exercises beyond the ones deemed feminine—dancing, ice-skating and riding horses—through a regimen of calisthenics.

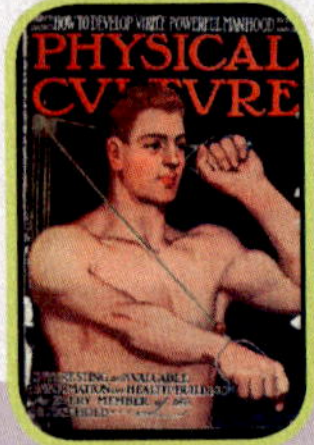

1899—One of the first exercise magazines, *Physical Culture*, launches in the U.S. Once a sickly child, founder Bernarr Macfadden makes millions telling people how to get strong.

1915—The U.S. surgeon general's office finds exercise "necessary for all except those actually and acutely physically ill, at all ages, for both sexes, daily, in amount just short of fatigue." A similar recommendation exists today.

1939—A landmark study contradicts centuries of advice against strenuous exercise, citing the good health and longevity of hard-working oarsmen at Oxford and Cambridge universities.

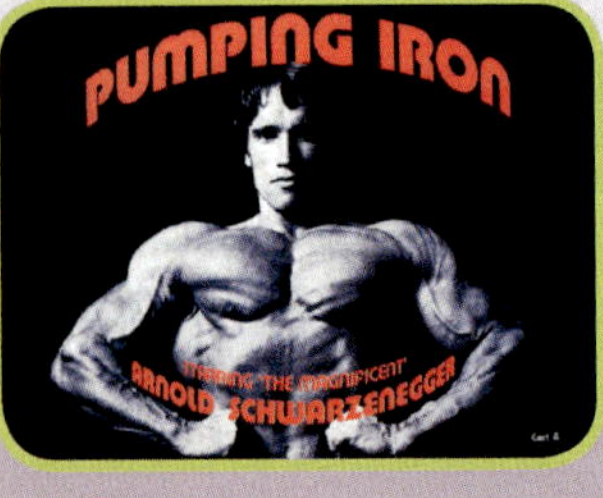

1977—Arnold Schwarzenegger stars in *Pumping Iron*, a film about competitive bodybuilding that boosts the sport's popularity and fuels the rise of gym culture in the U.S.

1982—Jane Fonda releases her first workout video, and exercise officially becomes fashionable. The series goes on to sell 17 million copies.

400 B.C.—Hippocrates endorses walking, wrestling, push-ups and shadow boxing to prevent disease, build bone and muscle mass, and improve digestion.

A.D. 200—Roman philosopher Celsus says reading aloud is exercise; he advises stopping at the point of sweating.

200—Hua Tuo describes "frolic exercises" based on deer, tigers, bears, cranes and monkeys as a way to delay aging and feel lighter. These become the roots of tai chi.

1769—"Of all the causes which conspire to render the life of man short and miserable, none have greater influence than the want of proper Exercise," writes Scottish doctor William Buchan.

1772—English physician William Heberden claims his patient with chest pain was "nearly cured" by sawing wood for 30 minutes a day.

1780—Exercise is discovered to be useful for rehabilitation after surgery or stroke.

1839—A prominent American health expert, Sylvester Graham, declares that you have to enjoy exercise for it to be beneficial.

1844—The first YMCA opens in London as part of the "muscular Christianity" movement, which emphasized the spiritual and moral benefits of fitness.

1951—*The Jack LaLanne Show* familiarizes Americans with exercise equipment, aerobics and weight training. It runs for more than 30 years.

1960—President-elect John F. Kennedy writes in *Sports Illustrated* urging a nation of under-exercised spectators (he calls them "soft Americans") to get in shape.

2008—Wii Fit sweeps the U.S., promising users the option of doing yoga, aerobics and strength training in their living rooms.

2014—Marathon participation reaches an all-time high, and more than half a million Americans complete one during the year.

How Exercise Keeps You Young

There are countless things you could try or buy in an attempt to turn back the clock. But your best bet? Working out

BY ALICE PARK

THE ELUSIVE ELIXIR OF YOUTH IS SO CALLED FOR A REASON: were it easy to obtain, we'd all be imbibing it all day every day. The fact is, there's no lotion or beverage or superfood or ritual that alone can do much to alter the course of your body's natural aging processes. But the more scientists study the biological underpinnings of age, the more comfortable they get with the idea that when it comes to some kind of a silver bullet, exercise is about as close as we're ever going to get.

For decades, the strongest evidence that exercise is key to keeping youthful vigor came from long-term studies of heart disease in which people were asked about a host of things that are typically associated with heart health, including what their diet was like, how much they drank and smoked, if at all, and whether or not they exercised. Those reports consistently showed that people who worked out regularly had fewer heart attacks and strokes and lived longer than those who spent most of their time on the couch.

But in recent years, researchers took it a step further, discovering that not only does exercise keep you from dying prematurely—it also may help keep you young. It also appears to be able to slow the progression of degenerative brain diseases like Alzheimer's, which tend to worsen with age. Scientists now believe that physical activity can keep blood flowing steadily to the brain, which is essential for removing toxic compounds that can cause aging and early death of cells. Exercise can also reduce inflammation, a key disease-causing process that can promote the buildup of the protein plaques in the brain that contribute to Alzheimer's.

The benefits of exercise for longevity and youthfulness don't stop with your body—it helps the mind, too.

At the real cutting edge, however, is the emerging knowledge that being active has a ripple effect on the body, from the feel-good endorphins released in the brain while we exercise to the stress—the good kind—that it puts on the heart. It also helps lubricate the joints, distribute oxygen to the body's cells and burn calories, potentially staving off the upward climb of the scale that can accompany advancing age.

But there are other, almost imperceptible changes that take place inside a body in motion—all the way down to slowing how quickly we age at the cellular level.

HOW EXERCISE HACKS THE AGING PROCESS

To stay young, you have to keep your cells young, and a cell's age is dictated by its DNA. Too many cycles of dividing over and over again accelerates the aging process, until eventually cells peter out and stop dividing altogether. Each time a cell divides, it copies its DNA (which is packed into chromosomes), and sections of the chromosomes, called telomeres, get shorter.

It wasn't always clear how exercise affects this process. But Belgian researchers recently discovered a compound, called nuclear respiratory factor 1 (NRF1), that protects telomeres from getting shorter—and the shorter the telomere, the older the cell. Genetics play a role in how quickly telomeres shorten, as do lifestyle factors, including diet, stress levels and sleep. Researchers have recently discovered that exercise can play a role in NRF1, too.

For the initial study, the scientists recruited 10 healthy people to ride stationary bicycles for 45 minutes and took muscle biopsies from each of their legs before and after the cycling session. They also measured muscle function by testing the amount of lactate in the blood. Based on analysis of these samples, the researchers found that exercise boosts levels of NRF1, which keeps the telomeres from being snipped away.

"Think about NRF1 like varnish on nails,"

says Anabelle Decottignies of the de Duve Institute at the Catholic University of Louvain in Belgium, who is a co-author of the study. "You cannot change the nail, but you can change the varnish again and again. What you're doing is refreshing and replacing the old section with new protective molecules."

And with each bout of moderate exercise, she says, the protection to the telomeres is refreshed, thus helping cells remain functionally younger. "The protection is constantly renewed upon exercise," says Decottignies.

Getting physically active can go a long way toward keeping cells young, too.

Experts think it's possible that compared with the genetic mutations caused by carcinogens and other kinds of toxins, exercise-induced alterations to DNA are in some ways their opposite: the positive changes wrought by exercise are more like tune-ups, helping cells to work better and more efficiently. What's more, scientists have discovered that these changes occur even after a single 20-minute workout—and even in people who don't exercise often.

Juleen Zierath, a professor of physiology at the Karolinska Institute in Stockholm, tracked the changes in the muscle cells of mostly sedentary people while they exercised on a stationary bike. She and her colleagues also collected small samples of tissue from the study participants' quadriceps before they exercised and again about 20 minutes after they were done.

Zierath and her colleagues then looked at a series of muscle-related genes before and after exercise. Not surprising, at least to the scientists, was the fact that different genes were turned on and off during exercise and during rest. Zierath says she and her team are trying to understand the early messages that the muscles receive when you exercise, so that they can better understand what's happening at the cellular level.

The researchers were able to see how muscles changed at the cellular level by studying another group of people who also agreed to exercise at two different intensities over a period of a week. On one visit, they were asked to take it a little easy: they would cycle until they reached 40% of their maximum capacity.

On another occasion, they pushed themselves hard, biking until they reached 80% of their maximum. The muscle biopsies following the 80% sessions showed more RNA, which is the first by-product of gene activity, than samples taken after the 40% sessions. This suggested that a lot was happening—and a lot of good was happening—when people pushed their bodies really hard.

Having muscle cells work more efficiently is certainly no guarantee of living forever, of course, but more youthful cells are a critical way to stay healthy into older age and to slow the aging process. That, along with the evidence that exercise can slow the aging of cells, provides robust evidence that exercise can, in fact, keep us young (or at least younger).

ONE SIZE DOESN'T FIT ALL

Exactly how much exercise is needed to maintain your muscle cells' youthful vigor is still being studied, but experts agree that if you're relatively sedentary, then even a small amount of activity is better than none. Remember that in the first study, the people were mostly inactive—and they only pushed themselves at a moderate intensity for about 20 minutes. Pair that with other research about sedentary behavior—it's now clear that there are few worse things for your health than not moving—and it becomes evident that even a little can do a lot of good. If you're already active, gradually building up to more exercise, with increasingly long walks or more-intense sessions at the gym or in the pool, is one way to increase the benefit over time.

So while humans pursue the inevitable—and inevitably fruitless—hunt for the fountain of youth, there's comfort to be had in the fact that exercise is an antiaging strategy with a lot of science to support it. And it's available to you, for free, no matter where you live—or how old you may be.

When Athletes Beat the Odds

Six sportsmen and -women who prove that competition isn't just the province of the young

BY JAMIE LISANTI

IF YOU'VE EVER OPENED A BIRTHDAY CARD TO A MESSAGE that reads, "It's all downhill from here," you're likely at an age when, according to popular opinion, your best days are behind you. For athletes, that comes even sooner—anywhere from age 20 to 29, depending on the sport. Still, there are outliers, elite athletes who thrive at a time when science says their physical prowess should be fading.

Their success doesn't hinge solely on beating the physical decline that comes with age. All bodies naturally wear down with age—albeit at different rates, depending on many factors, from genetics to lifestyle. But because even the world's top athletes can't escape the bodily effects of Father Time, when their professional performance calls for speed, strength, power and agility, they must find ways to stay strong, maintain fitness and avoid injury.

That's where the mind takes over. For many of those performing at an elite level—including the six pro athletes in the pages that follow—it's mentality, cognitive abilities and pure willpower that propel them to excellence.

VENUS WILLIAMS, TENNIS

When Venus Williams, now 36, looks over the net at her opponent during most tournaments, she's likely looking at a player who was born around the time she started her pro tennis career in 1994. That is, of course, unless the match is against her younger sister Serena, who is 35. That's what occurred during the 2017 Australian Open final, where her runner-up finish showed that even after seven major titles—and a 2011 diagnosis of Sjögren's syndrome, an autoimmune disease that requires daily maintenance and can sap strength over time—Williams still competes against (and defeats) the best players in the game. To help her overcome illness and injury over the course of her 23-year career, she eats a mostly plant-based diet. To fuel her body for intense on-court hitting, she also trains with a mix of agility workouts, tennis-specific gym exercises and yoga. And when she's not practicing her forehands and backhands, Williams keeps her body—and mind—in motion with some free-spirited dancing.

TOM BRADY, FOOTBALL

You'll certainly see New England Patriots quarterback Tom Brady participating in standard quarterback drills, but the five-time Super Bowl champion is also known to go above and beyond the team's standard workout regimen. With the help of Alex Guerrero, his "body coach," Brady focuses on lifestyle factors such as sleep and rest for optimal recovery, as well as meditation for a clearer mind and better self-awareness. His well-documented diet—heavy on plants and low on inflammation-boosting foods—is another key to his success. Brady eats mostly vegan; steers clear of caffeine, dairy, mushrooms and sugar; and avoids nightshades, such as tomatoes and eggplants. His approach may be unorthodox, but it works: at 39, Brady is in the best shape of his life—and has no plans to retire anytime soon.

JAROMÍR JÁGR, HOCKEY

Since his NHL start as an 18-year-old in 1990, Florida Panthers right-winger Jaromír Jágr has thrived thanks to his physical strength and remarkable vision and scoring abilities. On his 45th birthday in February 2017, Jágr became only the second player in NHL history to reach 1,900 career points, and the traits that made his career in the early days are still in play. To keep in shape, the Czech athlete engages in a mixed bag of training methods, each of which serve a specific purpose on the ice. Resistance-band sprints help build speed and acceleration, for instance, while shooting six- or eight-pound medicine balls against the wall with his hockey stick translates directly to his punishing shot on goal. While he's known for intense late-night workouts, Jágr's exercise routine isn't the only thing that keeps him solid and stable. "He finds ways to be stronger with his mind-set and spends a lot of time trying to find energy through activating chakras [energy points]," says Panthers strength and conditioning coach Tommy Powers. Powers also helps Jagr with other training techniques, such as Ki-Hara resistance stretching and mashing, a combination of Thai massage and other practices that increase blood flow and promote recovery.

TACO
BELL
GOLDEN STATE
34
WARRIORS
24

RICHARD JEFFERSON, BASKETBALL

He may not be the marquee face of his team like a Stephen Curry or Russell Westbrook, but Cleveland Cavaliers forward Richard Jefferson is definitely in the midst of his best NBA years yet—at the age of 36. Though he saw some success in his rookie season followed by a seven-year stint with the Nets, it was just last year that he finally earned his first NBA championship ring after playing on five different teams in five years. What's more, his career is already three times as long as the average NBA player's, and although he's not the Cavs' star player—that would be LeBron James—Jefferson has been able to revamp his career and succeed against much younger opponents thanks to a Southern California–influenced lifestyle change. In addition to regular weightlifting and other off-season workouts, Jefferson started playing beach volleyball and doing yoga, two adjustments that experts believe have been just as important to his late-career surge as his jump-shot accuracy and dunking abilities.

KERRI WALSH JENNINGS, BEACH VOLLEYBALL

After two shoulder injuries, the three-time Olympic gold medalist Kerri Walsh Jennings wasn't sure if she'd be able to compete in the 2016 Summer Games in Rio de Janeiro. Despite those major setbacks, however, she was able to rehab back to world-class form by adding new methods to her training and preparation, all at the age of 38. Pilates, meditation, soft-tissue massage and even brain training—using Versus, a headset that collects and assesses cognitive performance—were part of her routine leading up to a bronze-medal finish in Rio with her teammate April Ross. Walsh Jennings's sessions with trainer Eric Weldon also focused on strength training and mobility (particularly in her hips and upper spine), and on-court circuits honed specific volleyball skills. Top sand players tend to be older than most pro athletes, and Walsh Jennings still has not shown signs of slowing down, even after an improbable five tours—and four medals—at the Olympic Games.

ROGER FEDERER, TENNIS

If you predicted that 35-year-old Roger Federer would win his 18th Grand Slam title—and his first in nearly five years—at the 2017 Australian Open, even the Swiss Maestro himself would've thought you were crazy. After a serious knee injury requiring a six-month layoff to recover, Federer pulled through to triumph despite it all. The surgery to repair his knee injury—the result of a freak accident while Federer was drawing a bath for his young daughters—was the first such procedure of his 19-year career, a testament to his superior fitness and durability. But while his work with longtime conditioning coach Pierre Paganini helped him regain his physical form, his strongest suit has always been his focused mindset and passion for tennis—mind over matter, as it were. Said Federer of his title in Melbourne, "Coming back, getting older, and people have written me off maybe, makes this one so unique."

The truth about WEIGHT LOSS

BY ALYSSA SHAFFER

IT'S NO SECRET: TO DROP POUNDS, YOU SHOULD EAT LESS and move more. But what you may not realize is that at different points in your take-it-off efforts, the key is to emphasize diet or exercise. "It's easy to get overwhelmed by all the changes we're supposed to make on the road to weight loss," says Donald Hensrud, medical director of the Mayo Clinic Healthy Living Program in Rochester, Minn. There are so many fitness apps and diet-friendly foods, he continues, "that often people take on too much and then give up altogether." Consider this your guide to a smart, sane and more sustainable slimdown.

Focus on diet to kick-start weight loss

"To lose weight initially, emphasize reducing calorie intake rather than increasing physical activity," says Louis Aronne, an obesity expert at Weill Cornell Medicine in New York. A study from the University of Missouri found that participants who attended Weight Watchers meetings for 12 weeks lost about nine pounds; those who just joined a gym shed about three pounds.

For safe reduction, experts recommend taking off about a pound a week. That requires a deficit of 500 calories a day—cutting out soda and juice can do the trick. But you'd have to walk for almost two hours to burn off that many calories.

You'll want a structured eating plan to make sure you consume fewer calories than you burn, whether by cutting down on carbs or shrinking portion sizes. "Whatever healthy diet you will adhere to best is the one for you," says Holly Wyatt, medical director of the Anschutz Health and Wellness Center at the University of Colorado. Meanwhile, move more: take lunchtime walks or do extra laps around the grocery store.

Rebooting your diet and exercise at the same time can lead to failure, says Susan Roberts, director of Tufts University's Human Nutrition Research Center on Aging. "If you make multiple changes, you can't do them all correctly. And it's often easier to adjust diet than exercise."

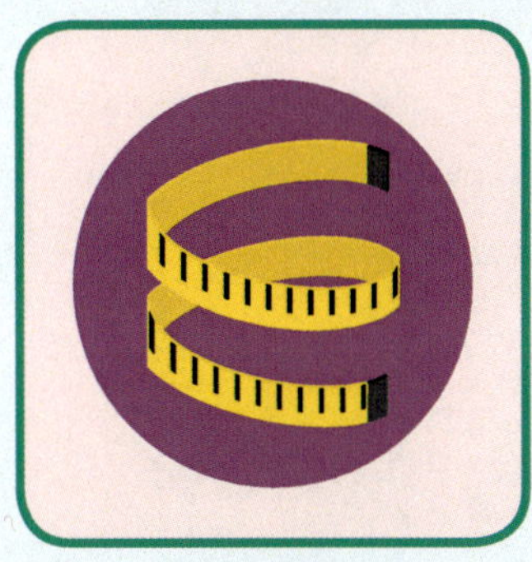

Eat and exercise your way to goal weight

Once you've taken off the first several pounds, combine your dieting with regular exercise, Roberts recommends: "In my experience, it's easier to work out once you've lost some excess pounds, rather than starting when you feel heavy and lack energy." A meta-analysis of studies in the journal *Health Technology Assessment* found that the combination of diet and moderate exercise for people on long-term programs yields the best results.

Cardio burns calories, but resistance training helps you lose fat, not muscle, explains Felicia Stoler, a registered dietitian and exercise physiologist. People who do only aerobic exercise typically have less muscle mass, and thus a lower resting metabolism, than those who pair it with strength training.

It takes an average of two months for a new behavior—like downing vegetables before a main course—to turn into a habit, research shows. Once you're past that initial hump, making better food choices becomes second nature, and bumping up your exercise won't be overwhelming. "This is a good point to focus on getting more physical activity during the week if you're used to doing so just on weekends," Aronne says. Schedule an evening walk on at least two weekdays, or follow an exercise video before work a couple of days a week.

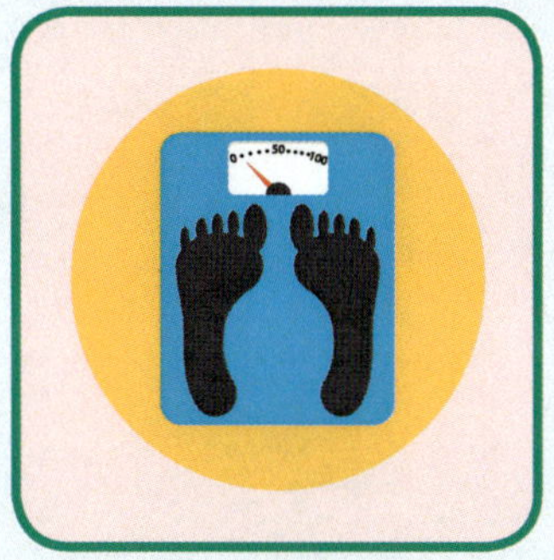

Exercise to maintain your weight loss

People who regularly work out are nearly twice as likely to keep pounds from piling back on as those who don't, according to research in the *American Journal of Preventive Medicine*. Other research shows that 90% of people who have kept off 30 pounds or more do an hour of exercise a day.

That's no coincidence. "When you exercise, you activate hormones that tend to favor using more fat as fuel," says Pamela Peeke, the author of *Body for Life for Women* and an assistant clinical professor of medicine at the University of Maryland School of Medicine. And, of course, continue to eat well. Regular exercise gives you a little leeway, Wyatt notes, "but it won't cover 3,000-calorie meals."

Of course, nobody can remain in diet mode forever—which is exactly why you want to embrace exercise as part of your lifestyle. As Wyatt says, "Emphasizing the positives, like how much better you feel, helps cancel out a sense of deprivation."

If that isn't motivating enough to cement an active habit, exercise comes with a built-in bonus: you'll likely miss it if you stop. "Being physically active isn't something you tend to just turn on and off," Wyatt says. "It becomes a part of who you are and how you feel"—so it's easier to stay lean for life.

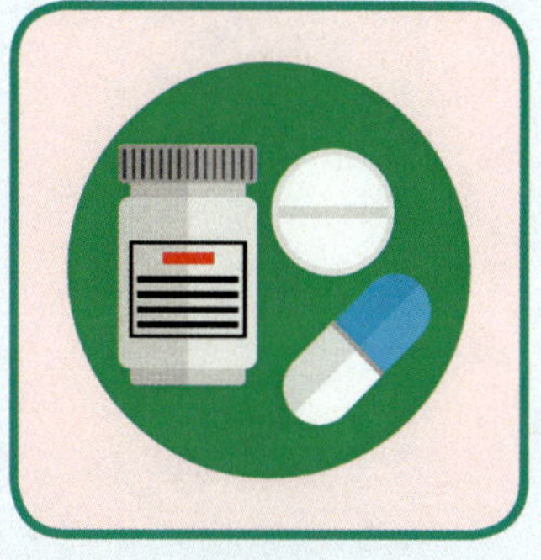

Dodge these common exercise mistakes

One of the most common mistakes is considering your workouts free license to binge. Don't do it; one recent study published in the journal *Marketing Letters* found that people who were told that a one-mile walk was for exercise ate about twice as much after the walk as those who were informed that the outing was for fun.

Second, use every spare minute wisely. Finding an extra half hour to slip in a workout isn't always easy—so have a backup plan. "Even a 10-minute cardio video on YouTube can keep you on track," says Stoler.

And no, you don't have to stick to the same routine every time. Don't be afraid to mix it up! "You can't perform the same exercises over and over and expect the same benefits," Stoler says. To get better results, follow the FIT principle: vary the frequency, intensity or time.

Feel free to switch up the type of exercise you do, too. Women who start an exercise program often think they should stick with just cardio, Stoler notes, but you need strength training to keep your metabolism revved up.

Finally, don't give in to your energy drain. A top excuse for not exercising? "I'm too tired." Fake yourself out, urges Wyatt. "Say you'll walk for only 10 minutes and you'll likely go longer. Exercise energizes you!"

choose your moves

Picking is the fun part. Your ultimate guide to figuring out your very best workout

The Power of Strength Training

We all lose muscle as we age, even if we stay fit. Here's why taking control of that is especially important for women

BY MANDY OAKLANDER

DR. DENA OAKLANDER, A PSYCHIATRY RESIDENT—WHO ALSO happens to be my sister—is the last person you'd ever expect to become a bodybuilder. She's naturally scrawny and a little bit shy, not the type of person to beast out at the gym—or so I once thought.

In medical school, she'd counsel patients on the importance of exercise and feel like a hypocrite, she says, since she did little but shuttle from home to the hospital, spending her rare free time catching up on sleep. "My body didn't feel good, and my mind didn't feel very good either," she says. But once she started taking her own advice, as a resident at Loyola University Medical Center, Dena quickly became a hard-core strength-training fanatic. Within a month of learning how to lift weights, she noticed she had more energy without needing as much sleep, she felt far less stressed out, and she saw her body tone up fast.

"Strength training is the only way you're going to truly be able to sculpt the physique of your personal dreams," says Sue Clark, a Chicago-based strength coach who trains Dena. "Above and beyond the physical changes, though, a whole new persona emerges as people start to feel really confident in their own bodies."

Clark saw the transformation in Dena, just as she has in many others. "Once I can get someone on board with strength training, they're good for life, because they're seeing results like they've never seen on cardio."

Strength training is efficient exercise for busy people, and many things count beyond pumping iron.

The average American flat-out loathes strength training. While about half of people do the recommended amount of aerobic activity each week, only 20% also do the muscle-strengthening moves that work major muscle groups. Yet the scientific benefits are stacking up in favor of it, from

Lifting something heavy is one of the few ways to make bones denser, an important perk for women.

bone protection to disease prevention, and it appears to have special benefits for women.

"There are so many misconceptions about strength and resistance training," says Larry Tucker, a professor in exercise sciences at Brigham Young University. "One is that you'll become muscle-bound"—so bulked up that your body becomes rigid. That myth was somewhat dispelled when athletes who started strength-training saw that they could hit a ball farther, jump higher and run faster, Tucker says. "Gradually we started realizing

there are benefits beyond sports."

But women in particular are neglecting strength training at their own peril. It's the only kind of exercise that makes muscles bigger, which lets them generate more strength and force, faster. "Muscle mass allows us to move," Tucker says. Young people tend to

3 WAYS TO GET STRONGER—WITHOUT LIFTING WEIGHTS

USE YOUR OWN BODY WEIGHT

"Body weight exercises can be some of the most effective strength- and muscle-building routines," says strength coach Sue Clark. A good gear-free option is to hold a pose like plank—or do squats, lunges or push-ups. Some workouts, like yoga and isometrics, naturally rely on using your own body weight as resistance.

USE RESISTANCE BANDS

These stretchy bands offer one of the safest weight-bearing workouts and come in different tension levels that your muscles must adapt to.

TRY A MACHINE

It's a less-scary option at the gym than picking up a weight or loading a bar. "Once you can figure out how to position your body in the machine, it's pretty foolproof," says Clark.

take for granted the day-to-day parts of life that require strength, like walking up stairs or picking up a baby. "But a sedentary lifestyle means that people are gradually becoming weaker over time," he says. Building muscle can fight back against that process.

It's also one of the very few ways to make bones denser, a perk that is especially important for women. Lifting something heavy, like a dumbbell, makes bones bear more weight, and in exercise, stressing your bones is a good thing (to a point of course). Bones are constantly remodeling, explains Anthony Hackney, an exercise physiologist at the University of North Carolina. "Your body is always adding calcium to your bones and taking calcium away from your bones," he says.

Sitting up and down in a chair many times builds strength, as does jumping.

This delicate balance starts to tip as people age, and "they lose more mineral from the bone than they're able to lay down," Hackney says. Over time, bone gets less dense and more brittle and prone to osteoporosis, a condition that affects about 10 million Americans—80% of whom are female. Women have smaller, thinner bones than men from the start, and after menopause they lose estrogen, a hormone that protects bones.

Strength training also comes with the less visible benefit of lowering risk for several diseases. "The only real way we can increase our metabolism, unless we take drugs, is to lift weights and maintain or increase our lean mass," says Tucker. Doing so makes the body more sensitive to insulin, and therefore more durable against certain diseases.

Recent research suggests that strength training may lower a woman's risk for Type 2 diabetes and cardiovascular disease. In a 2016 study, researchers from Harvard Medical School and the National Institutes of Health used data from nearly 36,000 older women, who ranged in age from 47 to 98. The women filled out questionnaires for about a decade detailing their health and exercise levels, and one question asked women to estimate how much weightlifting or strength training they had done per week in the past year. The researchers then tracked which of the women had a heart attack or stroke and which developed Type 2 diabetes.

Whether or not a woman did muscle-strengthening exercises indicated a lot about her health. Compared with women who avoided it, those who did any amount of strength training were more likely to have a lower body mass index and a healthier diet and less likely to be a current smoker.

They also had a Type 2 diabetes risk that was 30% lower and a cardiovascular disease

HOW TO FIND YOUR BEST STRENGTH WORKOUT

Strength training doesn't require a pricey gym membership. Here are three simple workouts with proven health benefits.

YOGA

Lift your own body weight and flow through intense poses, and yoga will give you strength with a side of mindfulness and stress relief.

WEIGHT TRAINING

A cheap pair of weights will build muscle and strengthen bone at any age. As an alternative, try resistance bands.

TAI CHI

These slow, gentle movements may not look like much, but tai chi strengthens the back, abs, and upper and lower body. It also relieves pain.

risk 17% lower than those who did no strength training, even after the researchers controlled for other variables like age, vegetable and fruit intake, and physical activity.

Not surprisingly, adding in aerobic exercise helped drive both risks down even more. Those who did at least 120 minutes a week of aerobic exercise and some strength training had a Type 2 diabetes risk 65% lower than women who didn't do either.

Most people should do both kinds of exercise for the biggest gains. But if you had to choose one, Clark advises, pick strength training. "Cardio is more digestible, it's less intimidating, but people also get less and less out of it over time," she says. As you grow fitter, you have to do more and more aerobic exercise to see the gains, she explains. Strength training, in her view, is the most efficient exercise for those with limited time.

Strength training may lower a woman's risk for Type 2 diabetes and cardiovascular disease.

Powerlifting isn't the only way to get results. Strength training comes in far more accessible forms as well—many of which do not even require a gym membership and certainly don't require a personal trainer. Resistance bands, cheap strips of elastic that loop around arms or legs, are one good way to build strength without weights, for instance. A 2017 study showed that when frail women over 60 who were obese worked out with resistance bands for three months, they dropped body fat and increased bone density. Another option that involves even less equipment is to use your own body weight. Sitting up and down in a chair many times builds strength, as does jumping, which uses many of the legs' major muscles. Even walking can count as strength training, depending on the intensity.

The right type and amount will be different for every woman (and man, for that matter), but a little bit every day will do wonders. Just ask Dena, who is planning to enter her first bodybuilding competition a year after picking up her first weight. "Not only do I look better than when I first started, but I also feel really confident," she says. "Strength training opens up your thoughts for more positive thinking."

Dena still urges her patients to exercise. But these days, it's a prescription she really believes. Not everyone will become a bodybuilder, but most can get stronger and feel better by moving just a little bit more. "I find myself really encouraging patients to turn to exercise as an outlet or a way to help them cope with some of the difficult things they're dealing with in life," she says. "The message is different now, because I do it myself."

WAIT ... THAT'S EXERCISE?

100

Number of extra calories per day a person can burn just by doing more active things like taking the stairs, fidgeting, singing and laughing

Heavy **gardening**, like digging and raking, counts as vigorous physical activity.

Doing **housework** a few times a week can reduce your risk of heart disease and stroke.

Standing more and sitting less is linked to a lower risk of cancer, diabetes and early death from any cause.

30%

The percentage by which people who move a lot during the day reduce their risk of early death—regardless of how much they exercise

Your Body on Exercise

Every kind of workout does something special inside the human body. Here, the secrets behind four popular types

BY MARKHAM HEID

Pilates can be done on a mat or a machine called a reformer. Both types will whip you into shape; Pilates sculpts stomach muscles more than conventional kinds of exercise. (Shown here: Chicago Cubs pitcher Jake Arrieta.)

Pilates: The Stomach Sculptor

PEOPLE WHO DANCE ARE EASY TO SPOT, EVEN offstage. "They're very aware of their body's position in space, and they move almost like cats," says Marie-Louise Bird, a Pilates researcher and postdoctoral research fellow at the University of British Columbia. "But most of us are more like puppy dogs, moving without much attention paid to our posture."

Luckily, the puppy dogs among us don't have to go to dance school to get better body awareness. They can just do Pilates.

Ever since Joseph Pilates founded his studio in New York about a century ago, the training method has focused on strengthening abdominal and trunk muscles—called the "core"—through hundreds of very specific movements. The first Pilates clients were ballet dancers looking for a way to improve their posture and control their movements.

Pilates looks deceptively easy. But the often-tiny movements improve balance and core strength, Bird's research suggests. Pilates does this in part by reinforcing the bond between mind and muscles, helping people engage the right muscles in the core. This leads to better posture and control over one's movements, says Cherie Wells, a senior lecturer in physical therapy at Griffith University in Australia. Wells's research has found that the core-strengthening perks of Pilates may also ease pain and improve daily life for people suffering from chronic low-back pain.

Some research has also linked Pilates to better flexibility, trunk stability, injury prevention and athletic performance. (Some former and current NFL players, including Antonio Brown and Martellus Bennett, are fans.)

It's easy to do Pilates incorrectly, so if you want to experience all these advantages, good form is essential, Bird says. That requires an experienced teacher, at least in the beginning. "Results come from a structured class taught by a certified instructor," says Ann Gibson, an associate professor of exercise science at the University of New Mexico, who warns newbies not to assume they can pick up Pilates by looking at a few online pictures or guides. "There needs to be a lot of focus on rolling down or up from the ground, one vertebra at a time."

The other unique part of Pilates isn't physical but mental. One of the key concepts of Pilates is "centering," or understanding that all movements originate in your core. "Like yoga, it's about breathing and focus and being mindful of your body's movements," Gibson says. At least one study has linked Pilates to enhanced mindfulness and sensory awareness, which may induce relaxation, mood improvements and stress reduction.

It won't surprise anyone familiar with the classic "hundred" exercise—a grueling Pilates pose performed for 100 beats—that the practice also sculpts the stomach. "Pilates seems to activate the deeper abdominal muscles more than conventional gym exercises," says Duncan Critchley, a lecturer and exercise researcher at King's College London. Research

Zumba, which brands itself as more of a party than a workout, has hard-core adherents. People who try it tend to come back because they find it so fun.

from Spain shows that Pilates also eliminates "asymmetries" in the abdominal muscles that line the sides of your torso.

It's probably not the best workout for those looking for a vigorous sweat, says Wells. Newer forms of the practice use machines to increase resistance and even aerobic intensity—reformer Pilates and jumpboard Pilates are two examples—but they're less studied than the traditional forms of the exercise.

Look around online, and you'll find plenty of anecdotal evidence that Pilates can help people lose weight or, even more likely, lose inches, though Gibson says her findings were mixed when it came to Pilates's ability to reduce waist circumference. But if you're searching for a mind-body practice that strengthens the body and has a few pleasant side benefits—like great abs and more poise—Pilates is certainly worth a try.

Zumba: The Most Fun You Can Have in Sneakers

ZUMBA WAS BORN IN COLOMBIA IN THE 1990S, quite by accident. A fitness instructor forgot to bring his usual workout music to class, so he grabbed some Latin albums from his car, ditched the constraints of a traditional workout and danced just like he would at a club. His class followed along, sweating to the salsa and rumba beats and loving it.

Since then, Zumba has pitched itself as more of a party than a workout. Indeed, some research suggests that it may be the very best workout for people who hate to exercise.

A Zumba class is like any other instructor-led workout, but with simple dance moves heavy on the hips and steps. Those moves add up to a decent sweat, says John Porcari, a professor of exercise and sport science at the University of Wisconsin–La Crosse. He and his colleagues studied women who were Zumba regulars and found that a 40-minute class burns about 370 calories, about nine calories per minute. That's roughly the same amount you'd work off if you ran at a slow pace or biked at 15 miles per hour for the same amount of time.

People work hard in class, too. "We found that they exercised at about 80% of maximum heart rate," he says, "and 60% VO2 max," which is a measure of oxygen used during exercise, he says. "It's a pretty good workout—similar to moderately intense exercises like step aerobics or cardio kickboxing."

But the most impressive part of Zumba is how much it appeals to people who stay away from exercise. A study in the *American Journal of Health Behavior* showed that when women with Type 2 diabetes and obesity did Zumba three times a week for 16 weeks, they lost an average of 2.5 pounds and lowered their percentage of body fat by 1%. More important, the women enjoyed the class so much that they made it a habit—very unusual for an aerobic exercise program. "After the study had ended, most of the participants continued going," says study co-author Jamie Cooper, an associate professor at the University of Georgia. "It seems like most of them had fun, made friends and didn't see Zumba as hard work."

The workout-in-disguise has unique physical and mental health benefits. Another study linked Zumba's hip-swinging, stomach-gyrating movements to increased core and trunk strength and better balance in older overweight women. They also had higher self-esteem. A related study on Zumba's psychological benefits found that people who practice it feel more independent and said that their lives seemed more purposeful.

It's easy to see why the activity would be invigorating and freeing. "You have to let go and have fun during Zumba," Cooper says. Dancing around others may help people feel less shy or self-conscious about their bodies.

The workout may be especially helpful for older adults who can't run or do more intense workouts (or for those who don't want to). One 2015 study found that even scaled-back versions of Zumba can help older adults keep up their cardiovascular fitness. More broadly, plenty of evidence suggests that dancing can help seniors maintain balance and coordination, lowering their risk for falls.

Zumba can never compete with more intense workouts like CrossFit when it comes to physical fitness gains. "But not everyone is the type to sign up for CrossFit," Cooper says. "There's still a place for Zumba, because people really enjoy it."

Swimming: A Whole-Body Workout

SWIMMING IS UNLIKE ANY OTHER AEROBIC workout because it exercises almost every part of the body.

First, the fact that you're submerged in water means your bones and muscles are somewhat unshackled from the constraints of gravity, says Hirofumi Tanaka, director of the Cardiovascular Aging Research Lab at the University of Texas.

This makes swimming the ideal exercise for people with osteoarthritis, for whom weight-bearing exercise can be painful. According to Tanaka's research on people with the condition, swimming decreases arterial stiffness, a risk factor for heart trouble. More of his research has linked swim training with lower blood pressure among people with hypertension. The coolness and buoyancy of water are also appealing to people who are overweight or obese, for whom load-bearing aerobic exercises like running may be too hot or uncomfortable, Tanaka says.

But don't be fooled: your body is working hard when you're in the pool. Water is denser than air, so moving through it puts more external pressure on your limbs than out-of-water training, studies have shown. That pressure is uniformly distributed, too. It doesn't collect

Swimming is a break for weary backs. Instead of hunching, the spine arches slightly in the water.

in your knees, hips or the other places that bear most of the burden when you exercise with gravity sitting on your shoulders.

You also breathe differently while swimming, says David Tanner, a research associate at Indiana University. During a run or bike ride, your breath tends to be shallow and your exhales forceful. "It's the other way around with swimming," says Tanner. "You breathe in quickly and deeply and then let the air trickle out." When your head is underwater, these breathing adjustments are vital, and they may improve the strength of your respiratory muscles, Tanner says. "This kind of breathing keeps the lung alveoli"—the millions of little balloon-like structures that inflate and deflate as your breathe—"from collapsing and sticking together."

Plus, who wouldn't want a swimmer's body? Swimming fires up more of your body's major muscle groups than most other forms of cardio exercise. "If you think about running or biking, you're mostly using your lower body," Tanner says. Swimming not only engages your legs but also recruits your upper body and core—especially your lats, the muscles of the middle back, and triceps, the backs of the upper arms. "You look at pictures of swimmers, and you see how the upper-body development is really tremendous," he says.

Even posture can improve, since swimmers' backs arch underwater. Working out in a horizontal pose—as opposed to the upright position your body assumes during other forms of aerobic exercise—may be an ideal way to counteract all the time you spend hunched over a desk or steering wheel.

The exercise is linked to many of the same life-extending, heart-saving, mood-lifting benefits associated with other forms of aerobic exercise. But it has an edge in the pleasure department. "People tend to enjoy swimming more than running or bike-riding," Tanaka says. While about half of people who try a new exercise program give up within a few months, people who take up swimming are more likely to stick with it, he says.

If you're sold on swimming, Tanner recommends starting slowly. "Don't try to do too much too early, and focus on proper technique," he says. Consider enlisting the help of an instructor if you didn't have any formal coaching as a kid. "If you're not used to swimming, it can be hard to relax in the water," he says. Being nervous and tight may limit the sport's benefits.

Begin with 30-minute sessions three times a week, and don't forget to take frequent breaks. "You want to ease into it and build up," he says, "just like a running program.

Yoga: A Mind-and-Body Warm-Up

WHILE IT MAY SEEM MELLOW COMPARED with most training programs, yoga offers health benefits that keep pace with—and often outdistance—those of other forms of exercise.

For starters, research shows that regular yoga practice lowers your risk for heart disease and hypertension. Yoga may also lessen symptoms of depression, headaches, diabetes, some forms of cancer and pain-related diseases like arthritis.

It might also help keep your weight stable. One four-year study from Seattle's Fred Hutchinson Cancer Research Center found that middle-aged adults who practiced yoga at least once a week gained three fewer pounds

Traditional cardio cranks up heart rate and stimulates the nervous system, but yoga does the opposite. Heart rate and blood pressure drop—and stress hormones go down, too.

than those who stuck with other forms of exercise. The same study found that overweight adults who practiced yoga lost five pounds, while a group that didn't do yoga gained 13 pounds.

How can a little bending and stretching do all that? Unlike exercises like running or lifting weights—both of which crank up your heart rate and stimulate your nervous system—yoga does just the opposite. "It puts you in a parasympathetic state, so your heart rate goes down and blood pressure goes down," says Tiffany Field, director of the Touch Research Institute at the University of Miami School of Medicine.

Yoga's various poses stimulate pressure receptors in your skin, which in turn ramp up activity in your brain vagus nerve, Field says. Your vagus nerve connects your brain to several of your organs, and it also plays a role in hormone production and release.

"Stress hormones like cortisol decrease as vagal activity increases," Field says. At the same time, this uptick in vagal activity triggers the release of the hormone serotonin, which helps regulate everything from your mood and appetite to your sleep patterns.

One thing yoga doesn't do, though, is burn loads of calories. Even hot forms of yoga like Bikram result in modest energy expenditures—roughly the number of calories you'd burn during a brisk walk. While more and more research suggests that calories shouldn't be your sole focus when it comes to diet and exercise, there's no question that running, swimming, lifting weights and other more-vigorous forms of exercise are great for your brain and body. Yoga should be done in tandem with traditional forms of physical activity, not in place of them.

Still, the research is solid: yoga is undoubtedly beneficial. It's linked to a healthier heart and has the ability to dial down stress, improve mood, quell appetite and improve sleep quality, Field says. When you consider the health perks linked to each of those brain and body benefits—lower inflammation, lower body weight, lower disease risk—you could make an argument that few activities are as good for you as yoga.

How to Beat Muscle Pain

There's such a thing as good pain. Here, some strategies backed by science

BY ROBERT J. DAVIS, Ph.D.

I HAVE A CONFESSION: I DON'T MIND EXERCISE-RELATED pain. In fact, I welcome it. The type of pain I'm talking about is soreness that comes after exercise. Known as delayed-onset muscle soreness, or DOMS for short, it's a sign that your workout is making you stronger. I consider it "good" pain. (Of course, what I definitely don't like is "bad" pain, which typically happens during exercise and gets worse afterward. It's a sign that you have an injury.)

Even if you don't share my affinity for DOMS, chances are you've experienced it at some point, especially at a time when you were new to exercise or picking it up again after a break. Any type of activity can cause this type of soreness, especially if the exercise is strenuous or something to which your body isn't accustomed, but DOMS is most likely to occur after muscle-lengthening, or "eccentric," movements such as lowering a dumbbell or running downhill.

For nearly a century, DOMS was widely attributed to the buildup of lactic acid in muscles. Today lactic acid retains its reputation among some in the fitness world as a pain-causing waste product. But science has shown that to be a bum rap. Our muscles break down glucose into lactic acid (technically lactate), which is used as fuel. Lactate is removed from muscles within a few hours after exercise, so lactic acid can't actually explain soreness that occurs a day or two later.

Instead, researchers now believe that the discomfort is due to the process by which the body repairs micro-tears in muscle caused by exercise. Soreness isn't the only symptom; swelling, stiffness, tenderness, and a reduction in strength and range of motion can also occur. These usually go away within several days, and when you do the same activity again, your DOMS will likely be milder—if it's there at all. And you'll be stronger.

Some pain can be a good sign—but you need to treat it right and avoid the hyped hope for what really works.

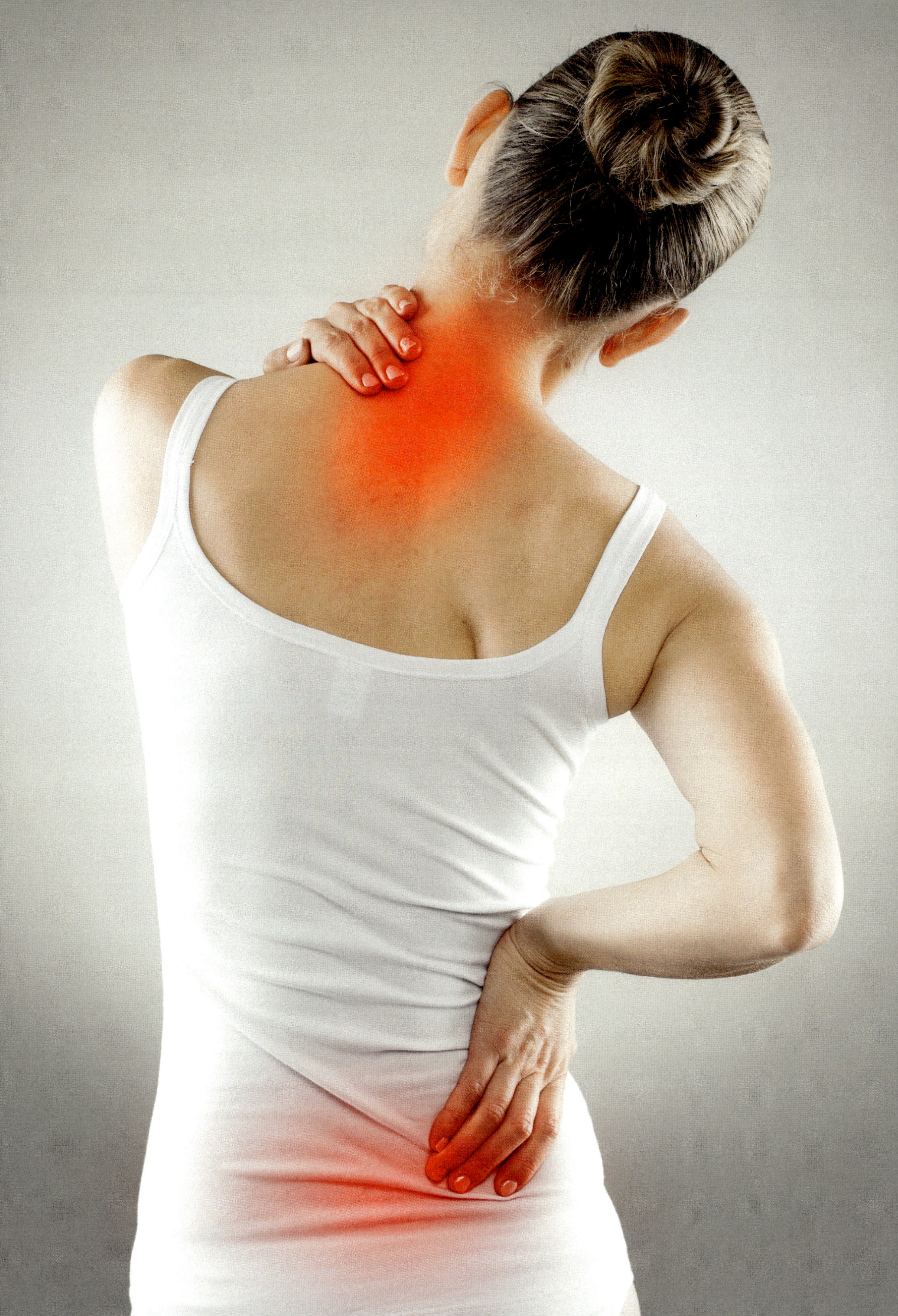

Heat therapy and cold treatments like cryotherapy have long been standby solutions for muscle aches.

Soreness isn't required for strength gains, however. You can have an effective workout without DOMS, so don't worry that you're wasting your time if you don't feel sore. No pain doesn't necessarily mean no gain.

It's generally fine to exercise with DOMS, though taking a day off to rest is OK. If you want to try something to ease the aches, read on. From heat compresses and massage to tart cherry juice and pills, some have more promise than others.

ICE BATHS, HOT COMPRESSES

Though heat and cold have been used for centuries to relieve pain, the evidence for their effectiveness at reducing DOMS is mixed. One reason is that different studies have applied heat or cold in different ways, at different temperatures, for different lengths of time. That makes broad conclusions about their efficacy tricky, if not impossible.

Methods of delivering heat include hot packs, ultrasound, saunas and warm water, which vary in their ability to penetrate beneath the skin into deep tissue. Cold therapy can come in the form of cold packs, ice massage or ice baths. In a review of 17 trials of ice-bath treatments, for instance, which are often used by athletes, researchers concluded that the technique may reduce soreness after exercise. But sitting in a tub of water chilled to 50-something degrees—ideally for 10 to 15 minutes—isn't exactly pleasant.

A relatively new method is whole-body cryotherapy (see image above), in which you sit or stand for two to four minutes in a special chamber where the temperature is as low as –300°F (no, that's not a typo). A review of four studies found that there's insufficient evidence to tell whether it reduces DOMS, however, and potential risks—which include frostbite, oxygen deficiency and asphyxiation—have yet to be studied.

The conventional wisdom, with little direct evidence to support it, has been that cold is superior to heat in reducing DOMS. To test this idea, researchers did a randomized, head-to-head comparison. One hundred young adults performed squats for 15 minutes and then received one of four therapies: cold wraps immediately after exercise; cold wraps 24 hours after exercise; heat wraps immediately after exercise; or heat wraps 24 hours after exercise. A fifth group, which served as a control, received no treatment. The verdict: both heat and cold therapy reduced soreness, but the cold therapy—whether applied immediately after exercise or 24 hours later—was superior.

Though scientists aren't sure exactly why cold or heat might reduce DOMS, it is known that the two have opposite physiological effects: cold constricts blood vessels and reduces blood flow, while heat dilates vessels and increases flow. Based on this, some athletes alternate between cold and heat, which they claim creates a "pumping action" of constriction and dilation that removes waste products from muscles and brings in fresh blood. Known as contrast therapy, this approach typically involves spending one or two minutes in a cold bath followed by a warm bath and then repeating the sequence multiple times.

Both heat and cold therapy reduced delayed-onset muscle soreness in a recent study, but the cold therapy was superior.

Pooling data from 13 studies, researchers found that contrast therapy decreases post-exercise soreness more than resting does. But it doesn't appear to offer any advantages over cold water alone. While it's possible that longer times in the water might yield different results, all the tub hopping probably isn't worth the effort.

MASSAGE

Getting a massage is certainly more enjoyable than sitting in a cold bath, and research suggests that it may also reduce DOMS, at least temporarily. In a review of nine studies on massage, six of them found that it alleviated soreness. The rub, however, is that the benefit generally occurred only in the early stages of DOMS, at 24 hours post-exercise. At 48 and 72 hours after exercise, there was less evidence that massage helped.

Though researchers aren't sure why massage reduces pain, possible explanations include its effects on inflammation, stress hormones or the nervous system. Another theory is that massage increases blood flow to muscles, though some studies refute this idea and even show that massage may have the opposite effect. Perhaps the most common explanation is that it works by removing lactic acid. But as previously mentioned, lactic acid isn't a cause of DOMS.

Because studies have used different massage techniques, it's unclear which methods are most effective. There's also uncertainty about timing and duration, though in most of the studies that showed a benefit, massages were done two or three hours after exercise and lasted 20 to 30 minutes.

One possible downside of massage is the cost. But self-massage performed with a foam roller is a relatively inexpensive alternative.

OVER-THE-COUNTER PILLS

Many athletes routinely take nonsteroidal anti-inflammatory drugs (NSAIDs), a class of painkillers that includes ibuprofen and naproxen, to head off pain during competition and DOMS afterward. Of the possible ways to reduce soreness, taking pills is certainly the simplest. But the truth about their effects is complicated.

NSAIDs, which are effective for relieving various types of pain, work by reducing inflammation. Since DOMS involves inflammation, it stands to reason that the medications would help alleviate post-exercise soreness. But research by and large has failed to prove that they do. For example, in a study of participants in the Western States Endurance Run, an arduous 100-mile race, 29 runners took ibuprofen on the day before and during the race, while 25 didn't take the drug or other medications. The ibuprofen users experienced just as much soreness afterward as the non-users.

What's more, when researchers analyzed blood samples from the racers, they found signs of adverse effects in those who had used ibuprofen. The most worrisome was mild endotoxemia, a condition in which intestinal bacteria get into the bloodstream. Scientists think this occurs because exercise and ibuprofen, when combined, gang up on the gastrointestinal system. Strenuous exercise can cause short-term injury to the lining of the small intestine, and taking ibuprofen—which itself can lead to gastrointestinal damage—may aggravate the problem, according to research. The result is increased intestinal permeability, which may allow bacteria to leak out of the gut.

Another potential concern is that ibuprofen and other NSAIDs may limit gains from resistance training. Studies in rodents support this idea, and there's a biological basis for it: NSAIDs suppress the production of substances known as prostaglandins, which are involved in the body's response to exercise-related muscle damage and the formation of muscle protein.

But several studies in humans have shown that up to 1,200 milligrams a day of ibuprofen (the amount you typically get in six over-the-counter pills) has no detrimental effects on muscle growth or strength gains, at least in the short run. It's still unknown, however, whether regular, long-term use of ibuprofen or higher doses can impede progress.

The take-home message is that the possible downsides of using NSAIDs to reduce muscle soreness on a regular basis likely outweigh any benefits. As for acetaminophen, there's no evidence that it causes gastrointestinal damage or interferes with resistance training. But unfortunately there's also little evidence that it reduces DOMS.

SUPERFOODS

It used to be that cherries were best known as pie filler. Today they have a reputation as a "superfood" with a number of health benefits, one of which is that cherry juice supposedly reduces DOMS. Though the research is preliminary, there is some evidence to support the idea. For example, in a small, randomized study, male college students drank either tart

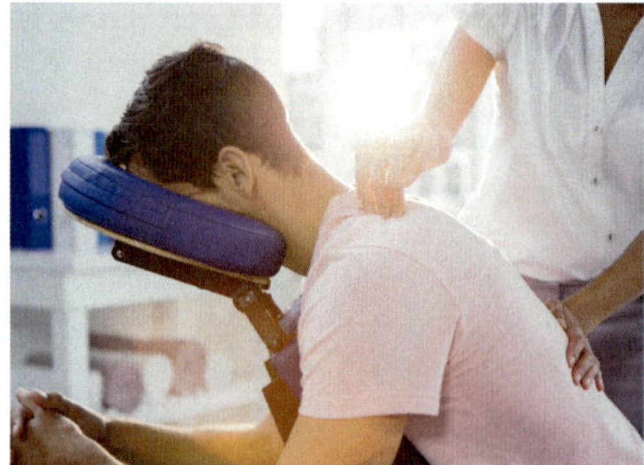

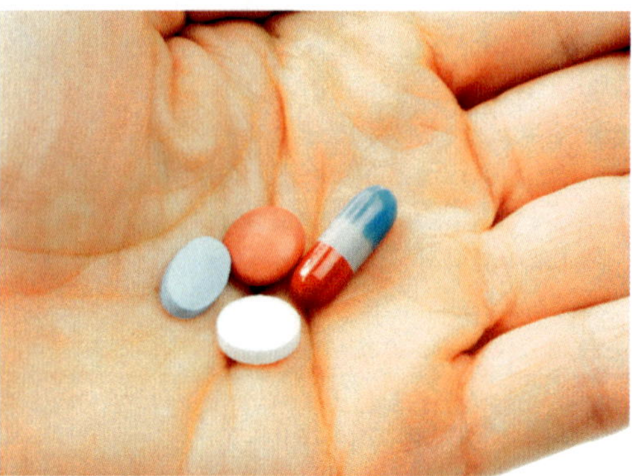

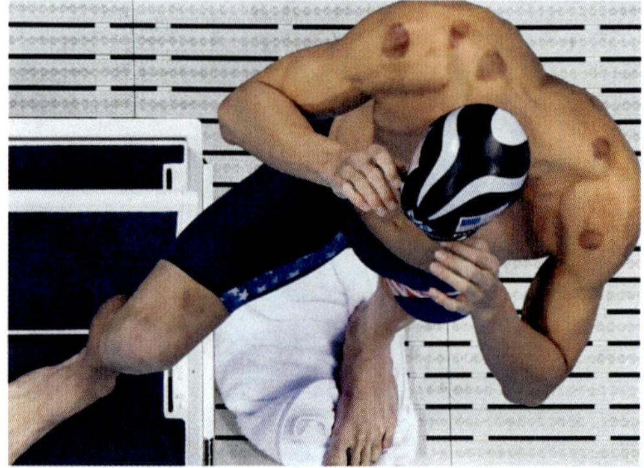

Massage, popping over-the-counter painkillers, trendy superfoods and even-trendier cupping are all popular pain-management strategies for delayed-onset muscle soreness—but they're not all equal in the eyes of science. Some treatments are more rigorously studied than others.

cherry juice or a placebo beverage for four days, did biceps curls to induce DOMS, and then drank their assigned beverage for another four days. Those consuming the cherry juice reported less soreness than the non-juice-drinkers, and their pain peaked and declined more rapidly. The research was funded by a cherry juice manufacturer.

In a study not funded by the industry, semi-professional soccer players consumed tart cherry concentrate (which was mixed with water) or a placebo for eight days. On day five, they ran sprint intervals. Post-exercise soreness was lower in those who had gotten the tart cherry concentrate.

But stopping there would amount to cherry-picking studies. Other research involving marathon runners and cyclists has found no reduction in muscle soreness among subjects consuming tart cherry juice or concentrate. Researchers theorize that differences in the types of exercise—and specifically whether they involved eccentric muscle action—may help explain the conflicting results.

As for how tart cherries may alleviate pain, they're rich in substances known as anthocyanins, which are known to act like NSAIDs and reduce inflammation. And research in rats has found tart cherry anthocyanins to have pain-reducing effects similar to those of NSAIDs.

Though the optimal dose is unknown, people in studies consumed the equivalent of about 100 cherries per day, which you can typically get in two cups of tart cherry juice or a smaller amount of concentrate. If you follow the regimen for multiple days, as was done in research, the extra calories and sugar can quickly add up. That may be a price for pain relief that you don't want to pay.

CUPPING

Although cupping has been around since ancient times, many people first learned about the Chinese healing practice when swimmer Michael Phelps used it during the 2016 Olympics.

A version known as "dry" cupping involves placing cups over the skin and using either a pump or heat to create vacuum pressure. This causes capillaries to rupture, resulting in purple circles that look like hickeys. In "wet" cupping, the skin is punctured before the cups are placed on it.

Phelps and other athletes claim that cupping reduces soreness and speeds healing, but the science behind this is skimpy. While some studies suggest that the practice may provide short-term relief for certain types of acute and chronic pain, reviews of the research have found that most of the studies are of poor quality, making it hard to draw any conclusions. What's more, none of the studies focused on exercise-related muscle pain.

Strenuous exercise can cause short-term injury to the lining of the small intestine, and taking ibuprofen may aggravate the problem.

Scientists suspect that cupping's effect on pain, if there is one, may be due to increased blood flow. It's also possible that any apparent benefits are in people's minds: those who report relief think it makes them feel better.

In any event, there appear to be no major side effects, especially from dry cupping. So if you want to sport purple circles like Michael Phelps, go for it. Just don't expect it to make you an Olympic swimmer.

The takeaway is that while some methods touted for reducing soreness may provide a bit of relief, none are guaranteed to keep DOMS at bay. With or without these remedies, you'll likely experience some degree of soreness after intense workouts. But don't let it scare you off or stop you. Remind yourself that the soreness is only temporary, but the benefits of exercise, if you keep at it, are lasting.

Adapted from *Fitter Faster: The Smart Way to Get in Shape in Just Minutes a Day* (AMACOM), by Robert J. Davis, Ph.D., with Brad Kolowich Jr. For more information, visit fitterfasterplan.com.

4 Weird Ways to Work Out

Exercise isn't boring with these four innovative (and downright wacky) fitness routines

BY ALEXANDRA SIFFERLIN

AERIAL FITNESS—CHRISTINE LONGE (not shown), THE AVIARY

I'm the type of person who is easily bored by group fitness classes. (I also hate cardio.) I've tried yoga, Pilates and spinning, but I always end up just watching the clock. One day, I learned about a local circus workshop and decided to enroll. I fell in love with aerial acrobatics and committed myself full-time to circus exercises. Soon my friends were asking how I got such toned arms. "All I do is circus stuff!" I'd say.

I then decided that more people could benefit from this type of exercise if it were more accessible—and lower to the ground. I bought several aerial hammocks (large swaths of fabric that can hold 2,000 pounds) and opened my first aerial fitness studio in Minneapolis. Using the fabrics, I developed a body weight-training workout that uses strength exercises inspired by Pilates and barre as well as aerial moves. I tell every new client that aerial fitness is not about getting skinny; it's about getting strong. When you're up in the air, you have to hold up your body weight and engage your core to keep a pose steady. That's part of what makes this type of exercise so effective. People are willing to put in the work to get strong because they want to be able to do the fun aerial moves.

People are often terrified before they go upside down for the first time, but once they get there, they always start giggling and laughing. Aerial exercises are something anyone can do with practice. I think that's one of the things that makes this type of exercise so special: people build up the courage to be vulnerable and try something new, and when they achieve something they couldn't do before, they want to keep coming back.

MUSEUM WORKOUT—MONICA BILL BARNES (right), ANNA BASS (left) AND ROBERT SAENZ DE VITERI, MONICA BILL BARNES & COMPANY

Three years ago, our dance company was approached by the Metropolitan Museum of Art in New York to create a performance for the museum. It was an incredible opportunity, and we decided to try something different: we developed a workout that the public could do while walking throughout the museum, looking at art. The museum agreed, and the Met Workout was born.

During the 45-minute workout, held before the museum opens to the public, we lead people around the Met with exercises like speed walking, arm pumping and squats. Our route spans two miles, with stops at around 13 pieces of art. We play fun music as well as narrations about the art. It's equal parts workout, performance and guided tour. All the movements in the Met Workout are easy to follow, but people still work up a sweat.

Though we are classically trained dancers, and not aerobics instructors or exercise fanatics, we spend a lot of time being physical and finding unique ways to use the space around us. We've always loved the idea that physical activity can open us up to perceiving things in different ways, which is why we wanted to make the experience of visiting a museum even more special.

The response has been incredible. The workouts sell out quickly, and so far males and females ages 12 to 86 have joined in the fun. Just the fact that this type of experience exists feels revolutionary.

UNDERWATER CYCLING— ESTHER GAUTHIER, AQUA STUDIO

I am originally from France, and about five years ago I took an aqua cycling class in Paris and fell completely in love with it. I used to swim growing up, and I thought it was brilliant to put a bike in the water and work out in the pool in a different way.

I decided to open my own underwater cycling studio in New York, to see if other people liked it. At AQUA Studio, our bikes are submerged in four feet of water, and we offer a variety of workouts that range from interval training to restorative classes.

Water has natural healing properties, which is why it's so healthy to work out in the pool. Compared with cycling on land, cycling in the water is a full-body workout. While we pedal, we also practice some swimming strokes, so people work their legs and their arms at the same time. The water also provides a lot of resistance that you don't get from normal biking.

Underwater cycling is actually inspired by physical therapy techniques. People who are injured often undergo rehabilitation in the water since it puts less pressure on their muscles and joints. Water is also more forgiving because it supports your body weight.

What I like about cycling in the water is the natural massage you get as you pedal. Being in the water also makes exercise really fun, and it's the type of exercise people can do every single day if they want.

Best of all, I love how happy people are after class. I think this comes from how therapeutic the water it is. Often people arrive at the studio stressed out about work or their commute, but once they're in the water, they release a lot of tension. Trying a new type of fitness like this can be intimidating, but I always tell people that this type of exercise is first and foremost about feeling good.

TRAMPOLINE WORKOUTS—LOUIS CORAGGIO, TRAMPOLEAN

Growing up in Lindenhurst on Long Island, New York, I always loved bouncing up and down on the trampoline in my backyard. Years later, I discovered there was a way to teach fitness classes using small trampolines, and I opened my own trampoline fitness company, called trampoLEAN.

During my classes, people are on a trampoline for a full 50 minutes. We may do some low jumping for a couple minutes, then some push-ups, followed by some balance moves. It's not an easy workout, but people have a great time when they let loose and have fun.

Sometimes people worry that they will get injured on a trampoline. But the trampolines in my classes are very safe and low to the ground. The workouts are actually lower-impact than other types of exercises, such as running.

Trampoline workouts help circulate blood and oxygen to all the tissues in the body, including the brain. They're also calorie scorchers, and the repetitive movements of jumping up and down build healthy muscle.

Most importantly, trampoline workouts are really fun. They take you back to the happy days of being a kid—which feels good for both the body and the mind.

JUMP
JUMP
JUMP

The truth about RUNNING

BY ALEXANDRA SIFFERLIN

THERE'S NO DENYING THAT RUNNING IS ONE OF THE MOST democratic ways to work out: you can do it anytime, anywhere, and all you need is a good pair of running shoes and some stamina. It's no wonder, then, that more and more Americans are adopting the sport—and doing it competitively: the number of people who finished organized races grew 300% in the U.S. from 1990 to 2013, and in 2015, there were slightly more than 17 million Americans who ran in races nationwide.

Still, estimates suggest that 79% of runners will get injured at some point, a statistic that's remained relatively stable for more than 40 years. "Running is hard on the wheels, especially if you're doing long-distance running," says James O'Keefe, a cardiologist at St. Luke's Mid America Heart Institute in Kansas City and a former runner. "A lot of people will break down orthopedically."

Since more than 80 million Americans are living a sedentary lifestyle, there are certainly plenty of people who could benefit from running rather than doing nothing at all—and if you do run already, there is no reason to stop unless a doctor tells you to. The latest science on running and its effects on the body offers both encouraging—and cautionary—takeaways for people who enjoy the sport.

More is definitely not better

Historians believe that our ability to run for long distances came out of our need to hunt (and run from) animals that could leap and gallop, but even competitive running dates back almost 4,000 years.

But running numerous races in a single year is a modern pastime, and researchers say that while running can improve health, at a certain point the benefits can diminish. In a 2015 review published in the journal *Current Sports Medicine Reports*, Carl Lavie, a cardiologist at the University of Queensland School of Medicine in New Orleans, analyzed large data sets of runners over time. He found that the runners had a 44% lower risk of dying during the study time and added an average of six years to their life compared with non-runners.

But how much people ran mattered. Men and women gained the lifesaving benefits of running if they ran at slow to moderate speeds for about one to two hours a week. The people in the study who ran the most, however, had worse survival rates compared with the runners who ran less and people who didn't run at all.

"There are people who get mad when we show they might be losing benefit," says Lavie. "They think it's skewed or flawed data, but it's just the best data that there is."

Lavie doesn't discourage people from running long-distance races or picking up running if they're inclined to, but he says that for health purposes, a two- to three-mile run is really all a person needs to do. "I want people to know you can get a lot of benefit at much lower levels," he says.

Running may prevent some injuries

Running has a reputation for causing wear and tear, but new research suggests that it may actually prevent injuries rather than increase the risk of them.

A small study published in December 2016 found that 30 minutes of running lowered inflammation in runners' knee joints. In the report, researchers at Brigham Young University brought 15 healthy runners into a lab where samples of their blood and knee-joint fluid were taken before and after they ran for 30 minutes. The researchers then compared the samples with ones taken earlier when the men and women were sedentary.

The researchers expected to find an increase in molecules that spur inflammation, but they didn't. Instead, they found that pro-inflammatory markers had decreased. "It was surprising," says study author Matt Seeley, an associate professor of exercise science at BYU.

Seeley emphasizes that the report is a pilot and that his team plans to do the same study with more people in the near future. "I think, and hope, the data will show that running is good for your joints," he adds. "Although the results are limited, they are also unexpected and could be important."

Not everyone is convinced. "There is data on both sides of the fence," says Brian Feeley, an orthopedic surgeon at the University of California, San Francisco, who wasn't involved with the study. "We know there are some people who run all the time with no problems and others that have arthritis at a relatively young age." For now, people of all abilities should allow themselves time to recover post-workout.

It may not be great for women's bodies

Women make up about 57% of race finishers, and data suggests that the number of female runners is up worldwide. But men and women tend to run in different ways, and in some cases, that can mean more injuries for women.

Stephen Messier, director of the J.B. Snow Biomechanics Laboratory at Wake Forest University, is trying to understand why female runners get injured more often than men. So far he's found that women tend to have higher arches and point their toes out more as they run. "We don't know if those differences attribute to a greater risk for injury," says Messier, but his team is trying to find out.

Prior research has found that female runners are more likely to be heel strikers, which some experts think increases risk of injury because of higher-impact landings. The way people's hips and knees are naturally aligned may also increase their risk. Women also tend to have less strength in their core and hips, which could affect them.

That shouldn't deter women from running, however. Women have more body fat, which is beneficial for energy storage and endurance, and they're typically more flexible than men, which can benefit their muscles. Women also appear to be better at pacing themselves during races compared with men.

To prevent heel striking, experts suggest that people try landing closer to their midfoot or landing softer during each stride. Messier is also launching a trial that puts female runners through strength-training exercises to see if some bulking up can help them lower their injury risk overall.

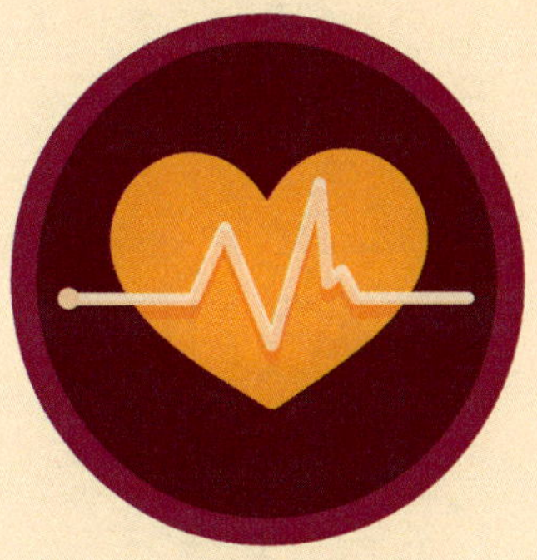

You can run even in old age—to a point

As the popularity of competitive running increases, more people are doing it later in life, too. "Generations before us weren't doing this," says O'Keefe. "People weren't running over 10 miles a day into their 60s."

Today, people age 40 and up make up nearly 50% of marathon finishers in the U.S., whereas in 1980, they made up just 26%. O'Keefe says there is no definite age cutoff at which running is no longer good for you, but curbing it with age may be a good idea. "Many people find that their joints feel better if they do brisk walking rather than running after age 45 or 50," he says. "I do advise people over age 45 to avoid chronic very-high-intensity long-distance running, as the body is not as resilient as we get older."

One study looked at marathon runners and their non-runner spouses and found that the runners were thinner and had lower blood pressure and heart rate. But the findings also showed that the older racers had a lot of plaque in their arteries and scored higher on a measurement of heart-attack risk.

Other types of exercise, like high-intensity interval training and strength-based exercises, are good to mix in as you age. Pilates and yoga have also been shown to improve flexibility and balance, which are important for runners—and in aging. "If people tell me they are running 25 miles a week, I ask: Why are you doing it?" says O'Keefe. "If it's to relax, be social or for long-term health, I tell them you're better off running a mile and a half and then going to a yoga class. Concentrating on one thing can hurt in the long run."

make it stick

No matter how busy you are, you can turn fitness into an everyday lifestyle

7 Ways to Motivate Yourself to Exercise

It's not just you. Here's how people get inspired to move—even when they don't feel like it

BY MANDY OAKLANDER

THE HARDEST PART OF ANY WORKOUT REGIMEN IS GETTING started (or, as yoga teachers like to say: "Showing up is the toughest pose we will do all day!"). It's a cliché because it's true, but even once you've pushed past your own excuses—*Too busy! Too tired! Too lazy!*—and showed up to exercise, there's still the challenge of keeping with it.

It's so common a challenge that social and behavioral scientists have been working on a fix for years. Luckily, it's a problem with many solutions. See which science-backed tips have worked for other people—and will probably work for you, too.

1. FORGET HOW GOOD IT IS FOR YOUR HEALTH

Dodging a heart attack that may or may not happen 10 years from now isn't likely to make you want to work out, says Michelle Segar, director of the Sport, Health, and Activity Research and Policy Center at the University of Michigan and the author of *No Sweat: How the Simple Science of Motivation Can Bring You a Lifetime of Fitness*. Exercising for eventual health is a worthy pursuit, but it's too abstract and far off to keep most people motivated, Segar says. "Those reasons just don't make exercise sufficiently relevant to our daily lives for the majority of people to stay motivated." Instead, Segar says, focus on what you'll get out of exercise

For motivation, focus on the immediate benefits—not the long-term gains.

right now—a boost in energy and mood, improved sleep or productivity—since those are the most motivating rewards of all.

2. PICK SOMETHING YOU LIKE

Many people feel that if exercise doesn't hurt or doesn't in some way feel like punishment, it's not worth doing. But while the workout you find especially tough may burn more calories and get more results in the short term, Segar says, it can be the hardest kind of routine to stick with. Studies have shown that when women try to commit long-term to an exercise routine, how much they enjoy it is a very strong predictor of whether they'll stick with it—and whether they will keep off any weight lost while doing it—in the future.

Choosing an easier, more enjoyable workout is far better for turning exercise into a routine they will maintain.

3. MAKE IT NON-NEGOTIABLE

The most consistent exercisers seem to be those who turn exercise into a specific type of habit—one triggered by a cue, like hearing your morning alarm and going to the gym without thinking about it, or getting stressed and immediately deciding to exercise.

"It's not something you have to deliberate about; you don't have to consider the pros and cons of going to the gym after work," explains Alison Phillips, an assistant professor of psychology at Iowa State University and author of a recent study on the topic published in the journal *Health Psychology*. Instead, it's an automatic decision instigated by your own internal or environmental triggers.

People with this type of habit, Phillips and her colleagues found, were far more likely than people without it to exercise over the monthlong study. Best of all, the more they

Doing something you enjoy—as opposed to a super-hard workout—is a much better way to make sure you stick with your new plan. Another good motivator? A fitness tracker, when it's used to track progress and set goals. The main drive, however, still needs to come from you.

exercised, the more their motivation grew with time—turning an effective habit into one that will last.

4. MEET A FRIEND FOR CARDIO, NOT COFFEE

Working out with a friend can help keep you accountable, since no one wants to disappoint a pal who's counting on her or him to make it to the gym. Some research has also shown that exercising with a close friend gives people more energy, higher spirits and less fatigue.

To squeeze in workouts with a pal, rethink where you meet up; hangouts don't always have to revolve around food, coffee, alcohol or movies. Do an active workout together instead. When you share an experience like exercise with a friend, your connection deepens, says Segar. "Physical movement is a way to connect with the people we enjoy spending time with, and that's a very high-quality motivator," she says.

5. DON'T BACK DOWN FROM A LITTLE BIT OF COMPETITION

Working out with other people has its perks. But cutthroat competition is another big motivator for getting to the gym, especially if you're pitting yourself against strangers. So finds a recent study, in which hundreds of graduate and part-time, professional students at the University of Pennsylvania were put through an 11-week exercise program with running, spinning, yoga, Pilates and weight-lifting classes. Some people were assigned to work out in teams, and the dynamics were engineered to be either socially supportive or competitive.

A competitive atmosphere, in which people could track each other's progress, encouraged people to work out more across the board. People who were in the competitive groups went to 90% more classes than those who weren't, and the researchers found these strong effects regardless of a person's sex or personality.

Group dynamics have a lot of power over behavior, and that's because a competitive atmosphere makes people focus on different things than a chummy one, says the study's senior author, Damon Centola, an associate professor of communication and engineering at the University of Pennsylvania. In the competitive group, all eyes were on the most active participants; they were the benchmarks to beat. "As people were influenced by their neighbors to exercise more, it created a social ratchet, where everyone increased everyone else's activity levels," he says.

But people assigned to the social-support group exercised far less than those in competitive groups—or even those who were alone. In the social-support group, people who dragged their feet drew the most attention. "The people who were participating less would draw down energy levels and give others a reason or excuse to also participate less," Centola says. Centola suggests gathering people with similar backgrounds and interests, then creating an online group where people can track one another's exercise logs. That, he says, will give everyone a mutual incentive to keep going.

6. PUT MONEY ON THE LINE

People are motivated by losses more than gains, and they prefer getting rewarded now rather than later—two human quirks that can translate into a surprisingly effective way to get people to move more, according to a 2016 study published in the *Annals of Internal Medicine*. A research team assigned almost 300 overweight and obese people the goal of walking 7,000 steps a day for three months. Only their incentives were different. When they met their goal, some people were merely told that they had done so, while others were entered into a cash lottery. Those in a third group were given $1.40 for each day they met the goal. Members of the final group were allotted $42 at the start of the study and had $1.40 removed

Getting competitive can help support your exercise habit. Research shows that people are more likely to be motivated when exercising around other people who are also working hard.

for every day they didn't take enough steps.

People who stood to lose money met their goal about half of the time—more than any other group.

Other research backs up the idea that financial loss can be a powerful incentive for weight loss. Findings like these might be useful for corporate wellness programs to encourage employees to get healthier. You can also place a bet on yourself through websites like StickK.com; by putting up a certain amount of money—at the risk of losing it if you don't meet your goal—you may be more likely to succeed.

7. USE A FITNESS TRACKER

Wearable devices and fitness trackers gather real-time calorie burning and step-count data, which can be useful for meeting fitness goals. But merely wearing one isn't always enough to get motivated. Some studies show that people who wear such devices don't lose more weight than people who don't use the technology, and most people ditch them after a few months.

This may be because people expect trackers to do something they're not designed to do—namely, force them to change their behavior. That part's up to you, and there are ways to get more out of most fitness trackers by using them differently, says Catrine Tudor-Locke, a professor and the chair of the department of kinesiology at the University of Massachusetts–Amherst, who has been researching fitness trackers for many years. For starters, she suggests, don't change your behavior after taking your wearable out of its box (or dusting off the one in a drawer) and putting it on your body. "Live life as normal for at least three to seven days," she says, "to get a picture of where you're at before you start to track where you're going."

Next, when you do look at your data, check for improvements. Then ask yourself how you changed your routine to cause those improvements, so you can do it again in the future. Once you have a realistic sense of your abilities, it will be easier to commit to a long-term goal. "That dynamic process of monitoring your behavior and tracking it is where we want to go and is the most important learning that comes from this," says Tudor-Locke. "Not the digits themselves."

Confessions of a Couch Potato

A former superfit athlete turned loafer figures out how to find a happy medium—outside the gym

BY COURTNEY MIFSUD

S I HUFFED AND PUFFED UP THE SUBWAY STAIRS, TRYING TO catch the elevated train to work one recent morning, I was reminded of Mark Twain's wise words: "Exercise is loathsome." *Is it ever!* I think to myself. *If one of American literature's great geniuses didn't have to go to the gym, then why should I?*

I suppose the out-of-breathness could be one reason, but ever since I hung up my black belt—I'll get to that in a second—I've had a hard time getting myself back to practice. I wasn't always this out-of-shape, and in fact, I used to love to work out. But if you saw me today, you probably wouldn't believe that I'm a black belt—a black belt and a taekwondo instructor who, needless to say, used to be able to conquer far more than a flight of stairs.

Yet here I am, about to miss my train as a sprightly man in running shorts bounds past me up the stairs, onto the subway platform and through the closing doors.

How did I get here? I got here how so many of us do: my life changed, my habits changed, and I found it difficult, if not impossible, to marry the old taekwondo me with the me who has to run up stairs to catch a train to my full-time job. Let me explain.

When I began training in martial arts, I was just starting high school, and working practice into my routine was easy. I'd go to school, do my homework, go to taekwondo, sleep and repeat. I even had 9 a.m. sessions on Saturdays. Somewhere in there, I'd find time to eat, and since my closest friends all practiced with me, my social calendar wasn't much of a concern. I even skipped senior prom to go to taekwondo

After getting out of the habit of exercising regularly, it can be hard—but not impossible—to start again.

camp—a decision I barely thought twice about. I hurled my way through all the colors of the taekwondo rainbow, from novice white belt all the way through to black and beyond, eventually trading in my white uniform for that of a teacher. I felt like I'd arrived—and I hadn't even graduated from high school yet.

Needless to say, once I went off to college, I had big plans for my future career in martial arts. I infiltrated the student-run taekwondo club, quickly landed the plum gig of head instructor, and was determined to finally land the daunting 540 kick (which is also nicknamed the tornado kick, to give you an idea of what it looks like).

Still, my earlier dedication—and the schedule that came with it—was impossible to sustain. Sure, weekly training sessions plus mile-long treks across campus kept me active, but I wasn't practicing nearly as much as I used to. I also started developing other interests, including the one that landed me where I am today: journalism.

Over time, the seemingly inevitable happened: my zeal for taekwondo began to wane. Sure, I told myself that once I finished college I'd jump back into martial arts. But as is the case with many of the resolutions we come up with in our lives, I had the best of intentions—but then something else came up.

When I moved into my first grown-up apartment, a third-floor walk-up in Queens, New York, going to the gym was the last thing on my mind. I now had bills to pay and a challenging job with sometimes-long hours, and I had to put food on the table for myself and my boyfriend. So by the time I'd checked everything off my must-do list, my want-to-do list looked more like Netflix and wine than jump kicks and drills.

I realized that I no longer had control over my weight, and exercise would have to be the key.

Over time, though, my jeans started to feel a little snug. Then my favorite sheath dress was suddenly too short. At a certain point, I had to give up the "It must have shrunk in the wash" reasoning and face the fact that, like so many people (but never me up until this point), the reality was I'd gained a little weight.

First, like many people who want to slim down, I dove into my diet. I cut down on carbs, curtailed the booze intake, even ate the occasional salad. But my body wouldn't cooperate. I realized I no longer had control over my weight, and exercise would have to be the key.

Naturally, going back to martial arts seemed like the best choice. I was rusty, but I was sure I could still throw a decent kick if I tried, and I knew I'd look forward to going to practice every day. No sooner did I psych myself up for that, though, than I encountered what I'll call Barrier One: cost.

After pricing out the local studios, I realized that any martial arts program would break my budget. With organized classes out of the picture, I turned to gyms. I visited a few in my neighborhood and was particularly excited about one that came with a rooftop lounge and a steam room, but the monthly price tag there wouldn't work either.

When I finally landed on the cheapest gym I could find, I encountered Barrier Two: gym people. When I first joined, the ellipticals caught my eye, but after 20 minutes of trying not to trip over myself on the easiest setting while the woman next to me bobbed up and down on hers, I gave up, with 40 minutes left in the hourlong workout I'd planned. I wish I could say that I persevered anyway, but I didn't. The membership is on autopay, and I keep telling myself that I will go back, but I don't. It's not the machines keeping me away or even the smelly locker room—it's that woman on the elliptical and the others like her: those for whom exercise seemed to come easy. People like me, back in the day.

Somehow, in my taekwondo days, I never felt self-conscious. If someone next to me had higher kicks or a better stance, it was usually because their belt was a different color, and that taught me what to aspire to. At my crappy gym? Not so much.

Still, even though I'm ready to give up on the gym, I'm not abandoning my goal to get fit—martial arts does teach you discipline, after all.

I've found a new workaround. It may be a little unconventional, but science says it works: I'm working exercise *into* my daily tasks, instead of making it a task unto itself. I'll do some squats while I wash the dishes. If dinner's in the oven for 20 minutes, I'll do some jumping jacks or crunches. My boyfriend and I have also started following along with kickboxing videos on YouTube. We push the couch into the corner, roll out our mats and see who taps out of the 45-minute video first. (It's usually me.)

One of these days, I'll save up enough money to try martial arts again, and I'm looking forward to it—but I'm not going to drive myself nuts over it, either. Mark Twain, after all, died at 74, far exceeding the average life expectancy of his time. So I'll keep practicing my kicks in the living room, but that gym membership will keep collecting dust.

How to Exercise When You Have No Time

Sometimes less is more, according to leading exercise experts. Here's how low you can go—and still get benefits

BY ALEXANDRA SIFFERLIN

WHEN MARTIN GIBALA WORKS OUT, HE'S DONE IN ABOUT 30 minutes. Considered one of the pioneers of short but sweet workouts, Gibala, an exercise researcher at McMaster University in Ontario and author of *The One Minute Workout*, has dedicated his career to figuring out how little time people can spend exercising while still reaping the full spectrum of its health benefits.

It all started several years ago. Gibala was a busy professor teaching his students about the mechanics of exercise. But his workload, and the fact that he was a father of two young children, gave him little time for his own fitness regimen. It was then that he trained his lens on a type of exercise that had long been used by elite athletes but hadn't yet been embraced by the mainstream: high-intensity interval training, or HIIT. The basic idea is exercise that alternates between episodes of intense exercise and periods of less intensive physical activity, or recovery.

Now, as part of his ongoing research, Gibala brings men and women into his lab and asks them to pedal on a stationary bike at various intensities while he measures their vitals—things that would indicate their fitness levels. Through his research, he has shown that if people work out hard for short spurts of time, they can have improvements in their health and fitness similar to what they would experience if they did a conventional workout of 45 minutes to an hour. The key, he says, is to

Martin Gibala, an exercise researcher, with a study subject in his Ontario lab

Research shows that as long as you push yourself hard, small workouts can have big results.

exert yourself at your highest possible level during the active intervals. "There's no free lunch," Gibala says. "If you want the benefits of very time-efficient exercise, then you need to push hard. There's no way around that."

SHORT AND SWEET

In 2014 Gibala made headlines when he published a study showing that people who worked out at a very high intensity for just one minute at a time were able to improve their endurance and lower their blood pressure. The entire workout was 10 minutes long, but the amount of time the people spent pedaling as fast as they possibly could totaled only 60 seconds at a time—making it the shortest workout anyone had ever heard of.

In that study, 14 sedentary volunteers warmed up for two minutes on a stationary bike then pedaled as hard as possible three 20-second spurts, followed by two more minutes of slow pedaling. After the last 20-second interval, they pedaled slowly for three minutes, adding up to 10 minutes total. The people in the study did this workout three times a week, totaling 30 minutes of exercise.

After six weeks, the men's and women's health and fitness levels were measured again, and Gibala and his fellow researchers discovered that they had improved their endurance by about 12%, had better blood pressure and showed improved muscle activity. The men in the group also had improved blood sugar control.

Researchers are still exploring why this is the case, but studies show that even short workouts activate the biological processes that make longer bouts of exercise so good for you. The same genes and proteins are turned on, but they are triggered in different ways.

Researchers at the Karolinska Institute in Sweden have taken muscle biopsies of people doing HIIT exercise and found that when muscles are stressed during extreme exercise, certain chemical channels in muscle cells that regulate calcium are broken down. Since calcium is important for cell signaling, extreme exercise can urge the cell to adjust how it produces energy and make it become more efficient.

"What we found was a breakdown of these channels that was totally unexpected," says researcher Hakan Westerblad, a professor of physiology and pharmacology at the Karolinska Institute. "We have never seen anything similar."

In another of Gibala's studies, he compared the benefits seen in people who did one-minute workouts and those who spent 45 minutes doing continuous moderate intensity activity. Their benefits were equal. "I continue to be surprised and amazed by the potency of this type of training," he says.

People who worked out at a very high intensity for just one minute at a time improved their endurance and lowered their blood pressure.

MEETING DAILY GOALS

Most Americans do not get the roughly two and a half hours of exercise a week recommended by health groups, and many cite a lack of time as their primary reason why. That's part of what makes HIIT so compelling. While Gibala thinks people should aim to meet those public health recommendations, he thinks that intervals offer people another option. For his part, Gibala only exercises for 30-minute increments at a time, but he typically exercises six days a week, if not every day. That means he meets the government advice for weekly exercise, but it doesn't take a massive chunk out of his day. "If your choice is all-out exercise or remaining sedentary, I'd advocate for all-out exercise," he says.

Interval training, then, is an ideal way to get health-inducing exercise in a short amount of time. And while it may not be recommended for people with serious heart problems, Gibala says his workout method can be tailored to nearly every fitness level. Most of the people in Gibala's studies are sedentary, yet they are still able to complete the workouts and improve their health. Gibala points out that even something as simple as walking can be turned into an interval workout by changing up the pace throughout your course.

None of this is to suggest that interval training is easy, of course—nor is it for everyone. "If you enjoy continuous exercise and hate the discomfort that goes along with interval training, even though it might be effective and time-efficient, you're unlikely to sustain it long term, so you're better off staying with your current program," says Gibala.

The bottom line, say nearly all exercise experts, is this: "The best exercise is the one you like," says Gibala, "because you are more likely to stick with it over time."

—With reporting by Alice Park

Anyone Can Be an Ironman

How one man broke his 30-year sedentary streak to do the world's toughest triathlon

BY JACQUES STEINBERG

It wasn't long after the nurse took Bryan Reece's blood pressure that the doctor appeared before him in the examining room, his expression grave. "You're a heart attack waiting to happen," the doctor told Bryan, after an EKG test yielded results consistent with his sky-high blood pressure reading. "I'm surprised you haven't had one already."

A 47-year-old manager of a financial services firm who had recently relocated to San Antonio, Bryan admitted he hadn't had a physical in five years. And he had not stepped inside a gym or had an aerobic workout for nearly 30 years. His six-foot-three-inch frame—packed with more than 250 pounds—had a pronounced stoop at times. It was a nagging pain in his back that had sent him scrambling several days earlier to the emergency room.

Bryan had grown fat on a diet of dinners that featured too many steaks accompanied by too many beers, martinis or steady pours of red wine. "You're going to have to take better care of yourself," the doctor concluded. "Or you're going to die."

And what about his back, the reason for his appointment? "Bryan," the doctor responded, "your back is the least of your worries right now."

This was in January 2007. Less than three years later, in November 2009, Bryan Reece would find himself swaddled not in a hospital gown but a wetsuit, his scalp shrouded by a latex swim cap, awaiting the starting gun of a triathlon in Tempe, Ariz., nearly 1,000 miles from home. But this was no ordinary triathlon. It was an Ironman.

Bryan Reece spent three decades of his adult life being sedentary. Now he's completed three Ironmans.

An Ironman is an athletic odyssey that begins with a 2.4-mile open-water swim (the equivalent of about 175 lengths across a community lap pool), followed by a 112-mile bike ride (imagine pedaling from New York City past Philadelphia) and then, like some kind of sadistic joke, a 26.2-

LIFETIME
FITNESS
LIFETIME
FITNESS
LIFETIME
FITNESS
Bianchi

mile marathon run. All of this must be completed within just 17 hours.

Like so many other middle-aged Americans who have been read the riot act by their physicians, Bryan had been frightened into taking his doctor's advice to get into better shape. Among his fears was that he might not survive long enough to walk his college-age daughter, Taylour, down the aisle some day. In response, he had joined a local gym, gotten an evaluation from a trainer and begun to exercise on a regular basis.

But Bryan was part of a decidedly smaller subset of Americans—about 20,000 in 2009; 35,000 in 2016—whose sessions at the gym slowly but steadily progressed to this: the determination to be known as an Ironman. By 2009, one didn't have to travel to Hawaii, the site of the original Ironman in 1978, to achieve that herculean milestone. Like a small cluster of McDonald's franchises—though catering to a decidedly healthier clientele—the Ironman organization stages a series of such competitions around the nation and the world each year, open to anyone willing to pay the entry fee (starting at $725 for this year's Ironman Arizona).

How Bryan Reece went from an emergency room to the starting line of the world's most rigorous triathlon in 35 months is a story as much about his mental toughness as it is about his physical preparation and endurance. But even those of us whose athletic ambitions stop well short of seeking to exercise continuously from 7 a.m. (when an Ironman begins) until the stroke of midnight (when its course is abruptly cut off) can surely draw inspiration from how Bryan got himself to that Ironman starting line—let alone from the challenges he would confront in the many hours that followed.

INSPIRATION STRIKES

As his visit to the doctor led to regular visits to the gym, Bryan's initial goal was simply to feel better. But slowly he (and his body) got the hang of things. Those slow jogs on the treadmill, for 20 minutes at a time and then more, supplemented by sessions on the elliptical machine, led to next-level aerobics: spirited spin classes on stationary bicycles set to heart-pumping classic rock tunes.

PART 1
2.4-mile open-water swim

A turning point came after one of those sweat-drenched classes, when he noticed that a fellow spinner had changed into a bathing suit and was headed for the gym pool.

"What are you doing?" Bryan asked.

"I'm getting ready to swim," came the response.

"After that?" Bryan said, surprised.

"I do some triathlons," the man replied. "I *need* to swim today."

That night, Bryan started Googling triathlons and quickly came upon references to the Ironman.

I can't imagine anyone would ever do a race like that, Bryan thought. But he was intrigued.

He learned that there were triathlons of varying distances leading up to an Ironman. He was particularly struck by one described as "sprint distance": in this case a 400-yard swim, a 15-mile bike ride and a three-mile run. *Maybe I could do something like that*, he thought.

But in addition to his still-shaky endurance, he faced a few immediate hurdles:

First, he hadn't been on a bike in 30 years.

Though he had enjoyed swimming as a kid, he was not sure he'd ever had a lesson.

And as for running, that was a distant, un-

PART 2
112-mile
bike ride

happy memory from his days as a linebacker on his high school football team.

Still, a seed had been planted.

TRAINING TAKES OVER

In late spring 2007, Bryan found a 12-week training plan online. If he followed it, he would be ready for his first triathlon by September. And as it turned out, there was just such an event, at the starter (or sprint) distance, in San Antonio that month.

In preparation, Bryan bought a bike. He also decided the time had come to dip a toe, to be followed by rest of his body, into the gym pool.

Making sure he did so at an off hour, Bryan slipped into the far left lane of the indoor pool and began making his way across. He swam the front crawl as best as he could remember from his childhood. As the far wall came into view, he lunged for it. He couldn't seem to catch his breath and had no idea how he would ever manage to let go.

Bryan's next move seemed obvious: get out. But he recalled hearing somewhere that you never got out of a pool on the side opposite the one you entered—so he set out for the other side. By the halfway point, he could do little more than walk to the end. And yet, he was on his way.

Throughout Bryan's quest to get in shape—from doing laps to completing the sprint triathlon in San Antonio to going for an Ironman—he was determined to progress methodically and carefully, adding distance to his swimming, biking and running in small increments. He was guided by credible advice he found on the Web and in books, as well as through coaching provided by an online triathlon club.

For example, it was through the website of a running guru named Jeff Galloway that Bryan discovered a strategy that instructed him to run for four minutes, then recover with a walk for a minute, then resume running. With that approach, Bryan found he could ultimately go longer (and faster) than if he embarked on a steady jog.

Bryan began polishing off triathlons of increasing distances. Before long, his weekend bike rides were topping 50 miles, and he was finding that he could run for 14 miles at a time, then 17 miles, then 20 miles.

Bryan's gaze always seemed to be scanning the horizon for the next big challenge,

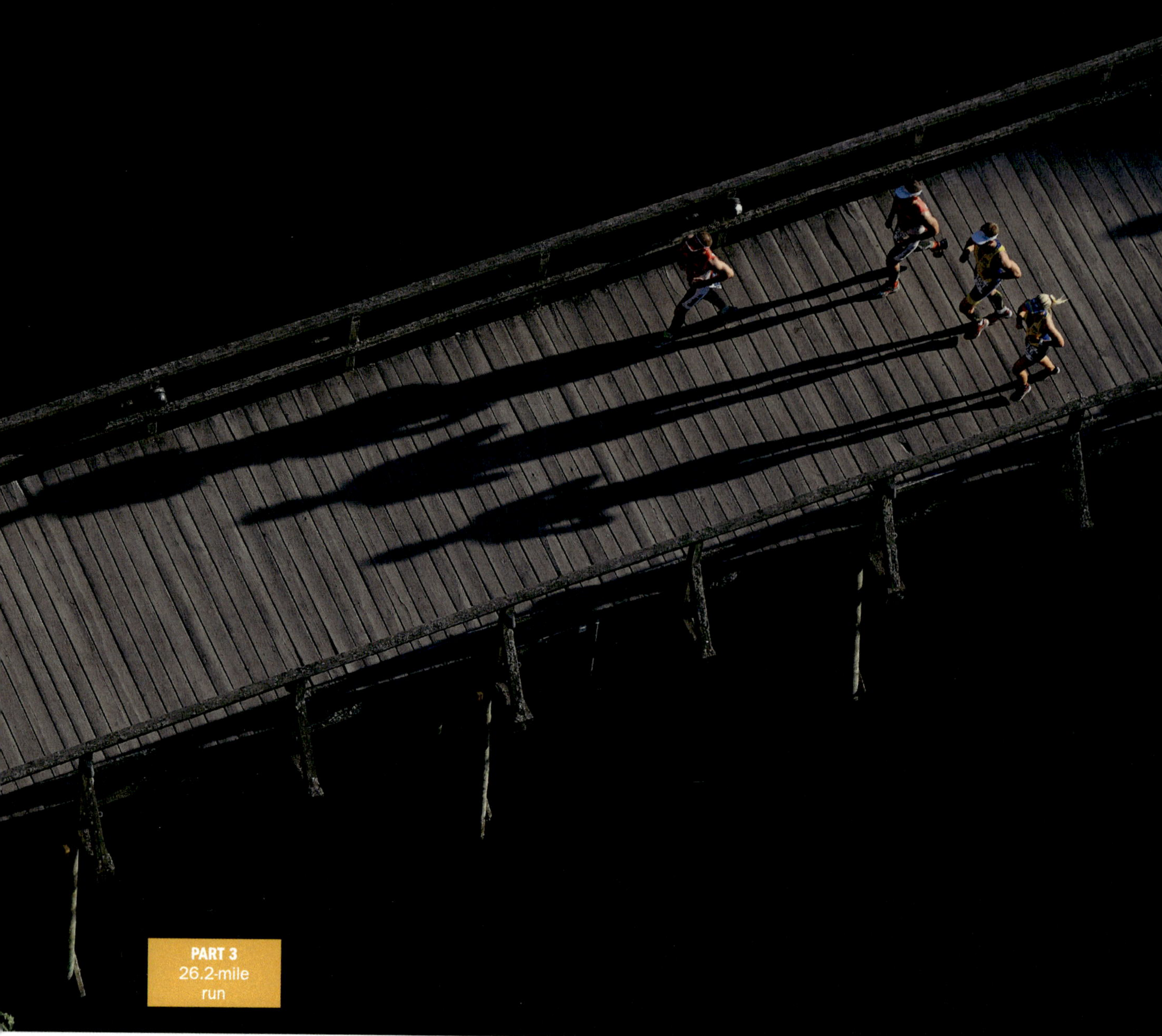

and the Ironman began to loom as a potential goal. Never mind that such an endeavor would force him to swim, bike and run more in a day than most people will do across the span of their entire lives.

The hours he devoted in a typical week to swimming, biking and running cruised well past the 10-hour mark, and Bryan realized that his mental resilience was just as critical to his success as the efforts he was making to increase his endurance.

After one 20-mile run, nearly two years after his life-changing visit to the doctor, Bryan observed that about "80% of the way into the run, give or take a little, the mental side begins to take control."

"There is no doubt the joints, legs, feet and hips are hurting by then," he added, "but the old nugget between the ears begins to rule."

RACE DAY ARRIVES

On the Sunday before Thanksgiving in 2009, as the sun rose, Bryan slipped into Tempe Town Lake with more than 2,500 other souls encased in full wetsuits. He was in many ways unrecognizable from the man in that doctor's office nearly three years earlier. His weight had dropped from 250 pounds to just under 220. He was no longer on blood pressure medication, and his back rarely acted up.

As crazy as it sounds, the race that would unfold over the next 17 hours was in some ways anticlimactic for Bryan.

On the 2.4-mile swim, which entailed swimming up toward a bridge and then back, Bryan felt an eerie sense of calm, despite the churn of several thousand arms and legs, some of which inadvertently kicked and punched him. Just under an hour and 40 minutes after the starting cannon, Bryan climbed a small metal ladder from the lake onto the shore, as Bon Jovi's "Livin' on a Prayer" blared. The first leg of Ironman Arizona was complete.

Wearing a cycling jersey and shorts, Bryan climbed onto his bike. Other than a few brief pit stops, he would spend the better part of the next eight hours in that saddle, as he covered three loops totaling 112 miles from downtown Tempe out into the desert, then back again.

As on the swim, Bryan felt well trained and prepared; among the biggest challenges were the occasional stretches of boredom and monotony. Periodically he nibbled a peanut butter sandwich or swigged from an energy drink.

One piece at a time, he would remind himself, as he broke the ride mentally into intervals.

It's all about one stroke, one pedal revolution, one step. You just put a whole bunch of those things together back to back to back.

By 5 p.m., Bryan had completed his daylong bike ride and had moved on to the run. He now had seven hours to finish a marathon—which meant that if he maintained a pace of about 3.75 miles an hour, alternately running and walking as he had trained, he could make the finish line before the midnight cutoff.

Though the bulk of the race was behind him, he thought, *I don't want to take anything for granted*.

Just before 7 p.m.—12 hours after the day's journey had begun—he approached the halfway point of the run and began to get emotional. He retrieved a greeting card that his wife, Debbie, had left for him at mile 13. "I know how hard you worked for this," it read. "I also know that if anyone can do this, you can!"

About a quarter-mile from the finish, Bryan began high-fiving volunteers and spectators, thanking them for supporting him and the other participants that day. Then Bryan spied Debbie and his brother, Bruce, in the crowd.

Oh my, Bryan thought. *Here it comes!*

Minutes later, Bryan heard the voice of the announcer say the words he had longed to hear for months.

"Bryan Reece of San Antonio, Texas," the announcer boomed. "You are an Ironman."

It was 10:45 p.m.: 15 hours and 45 minutes after he took his first swim stroke, and 75 minutes before the race cutoff.

Bryan thrust his fists in the air, crossed under the archway that signaled his race was over and promptly fell into the arms of a volunteer who had pushed her way through the crowd and into the finish area. It was Debbie. As they both wept, Bryan could muster only three words.

"I did it."

Like so many first-time Ironmen, he would strive to do it again. Bryan completed Ironman Florida, in Panama City, in 2010, and returned to complete Ironman Arizona again in 2011.

He also achieved the goal that drove him to get in shape in the first place. He walked his daughter Taylour down the aisle on a beach in Port Aransas, Texas, in 2015, and he was there to welcome her son, Tucker—his first grandchild—two years later.

Asked to sum up what that first Ironman pursuit and finish had meant to him, Bryan had this to say: "If I plan and strategize and put my mind to it, I can do absolutely anything."

"It's all about one stroke, one pedal revolution, one step," he said. "You just put a whole bunch of those things together back to back to back to back. And nothing seems that big."

Adapted from You Are an Ironman: How Six Weekend Warriors Chased Their Dream of Finishing the World's Toughest Triathlon, *by Jacques Steinberg (Viking-Penguin, 2012)*

The truth about WALKING

BY MARKHAM HEID

WALKING MAY SEEM MORE LIKE A LEISURELY mode of transportation than formal exercise, but it absolutely counts. "If you think about all fitness activities as a pyramid, walking would be the foundation," says James O'Keefe, medical director of the Cardio Health & Wellness Center at Saint Luke's Mid America Heart Institute in Kansas City. "It's what we've done since we evolved from our four-legged ancestors, and we shouldn't discount its benefits."

A stroll offers a surprising number of health perks. In a recent study of people who spent much of their day sitting, those who took breaks by standing or walking—even for short bouts—had trimmer waists, lower body mass indexes, and better scores on measures of heart disease and diabetes than people who didn't take those breaks.

"We've learned that breaking up sedentary periods as frequently as you can is really important, and walking is usually the easiest way to do that," says Sabrena Jo of the American Council on Exercise (ACE). "Even if it's just for a few minutes, walking makes a difference."

Here are four amazing things walking can do.

It lowers your risk for disease

"Pick a medical condition, and walking is probably good for [preventing] it," says Tim Church, a professor at Louisiana State University's Pennington Biomedical Research Center.

It can even pack the same powerful effects as much tougher types of exercise, without all the strain. One study found that brisk walking can lower risk for high blood pressure, high cholesterol and diabetes just as much as running. Another study of nearly 80,000 women linked a few hours of walking each week to a 42% drop in breast-cancer mortality risk. Walking is also associated with a reduced risk for at least a dozen kinds of cancer, including kidney and prostate.

THE SECRETS TO FINDING YOUR STRIDE

There's more to it than putting one foot in front of the other. Here are five science-backed ways to reap the most rewards from your walk.

PICK UP THE PACE

Whether you're an unhurried stroller or a power strider, "increase your pace above whatever's normal for you," says Jo from ACE. Think of it as walking with a mission.

COUNT YOUR STEPS

Walking 10,000 steps a day is ideal. But healthy adults should aim for at least 7,000, says Church—and "you want 3,000 of those to be with purpose."

It will probably extend your life

"If your goal is longevity, walking may be the best exercise," says O'Keefe. It may ultimately be better than running and other strenuous forms of physical activity, his research suggests, because it doesn't cause bodily wear and tear. (Another reason it rules: walking has the lowest quit rate of any type of exercise.)

"Most people conflate overall fitness—say, your heart's ability to handle a long workout—with health and longevity," O'Keefe says. But a simple walking habit can add healthy years to your life. One Taiwanese study of more than 400,000 people found that those who did moderate-intensity exercise, like walking, for just 15 minutes a day tended to live three years longer than inactive adults and were 14% less likely to die from any cause.

It may make you happier

Walking improves your mood. "We're finding more and more that walking is a wonderful activity for mental health, especially if you do it outdoors," says O'Keefe.

A walk in the woods, the park and other natural settings lowers stress and improves well-being. But you don't need to ditch civilization to get an attitude adjustment: a 2016 study found that a five-minute walk inside a drab office building can buoy a person's mood. Walking has also been shown to improve creativity, both inside and outdoors. (The act of moving, not your environment, seems to be what sparks inspiration.) Other research links walking to better cognitive function among older adults. "We've shown improvements in anxiety, depression, quality of life and just general well-being," says Church.

It can keep you limber longer

Starting a walking habit early ensures better mobility years down the line, when you'll need it. But even if you start in old age, it can keep you upright and on the go.

One recent study found that older sedentary adults cut their risk for disability by 25% by taking up light forms of exercise, including walking. Other research showed that when a group of seniors took two walks a day, they became nearly 20% more mobile in their daily activities.

It can also keep aches away. In one study, older people with arthritis who walked 45 minutes a week were 80% more likely to maintain—or even improve—their physical functioning, compared with those who didn't walk regularly.

All of this science proves the old saying: a body in motion stays in motion.

BREAK UP THE DAY

Even if you log a lot of hours in the gym, stretches of inactivity still take a toll. Go on a mini walk every 45 minutes: just 50 steps is enough, Church says.

GO WITH A GROUP

Research shows that joining a walking group lowers blood pressure, heart rate, body fat and depression scores—and once people start, they don't tend to drop out.

TRY IT MINDFULLY

Going for a mindful walk can alleviate pain (and it's easier than sitting in meditation). Focus on each small, slow step, and with every footfall, bring attention to your breath.

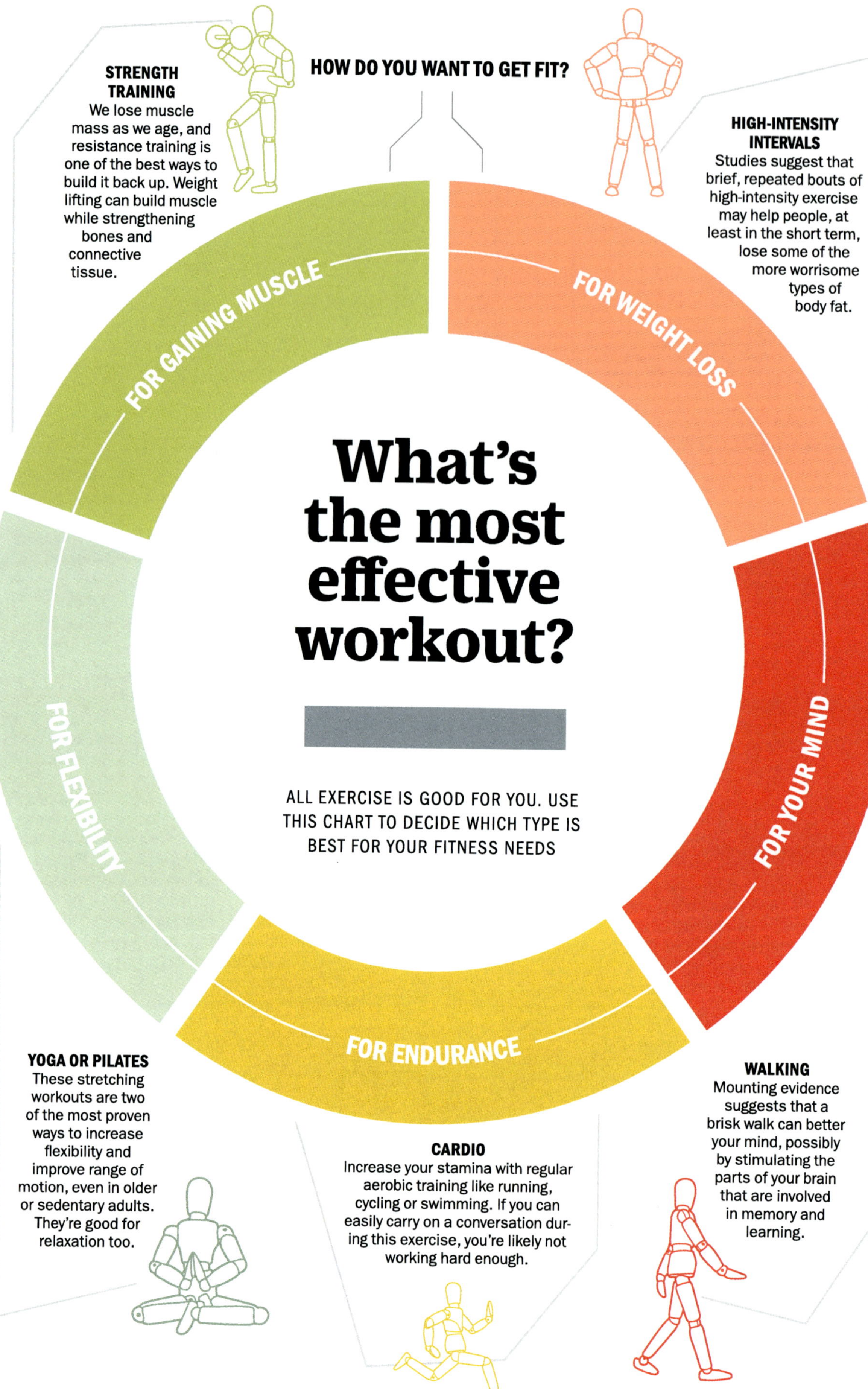
HOW DO YOU WANT TO GET FIT?
STRENGTH TRAINING
We lose muscle mass as we age, and resistance training is one of the best ways to build it back up. Weight lifting can build muscle while strengthening bones and connective tissue.
HIGH-INTENSITY INTERVALS
Studies suggest that brief, repeated bouts of high-intensity exercise may help people, at least in the short term, lose some of the more worrisome types of body fat.
FOR GAINING MUSCLE
FOR WEIGHT LOSS
What's the most effective workout?
ALL EXERCISE IS GOOD FOR YOU. USE THIS CHART TO DECIDE WHICH TYPE IS BEST FOR YOUR FITNESS NEEDS
FOR FLEXIBILITY
FOR YOUR MIND
FOR ENDURANCE
YOGA OR PILATES
These stretching workouts are two of the most proven ways to increase flexibility and improve range of motion, even in older or sedentary adults. They're good for relaxation too.
CARDIO
Increase your stamina with regular aerobic training like running, cycling or swimming. If you can easily carry on a conversation during this exercise, you're likely not working hard enough.
WALKING
Mounting evidence suggests that a brisk walk can better your mind, possibly by stimulating the parts of your brain that are involved in memory and learning.

The Science of Exercise

Editors Siobhan O'Connor, Mandy Oaklander
Designer Skye Gurney
Writers Robert J. Davis, Merrill Fabry, Markham Heid, Jamie Lisanti, Jordan Metzl, Courtney Mifsud, Camille Noe Pagán, Alice Park, Alyssa Shaffer, Alexandra Sifferlin, Jacques Steinberg
Photo Editor Dot McMahon
Reporters Elizabeth L. Bland, Andréa Ford
Editorial Production David Sloan

TIME INC. BOOKS
Publisher Margot Schupf
Associate Publisher Allison Devlin
Vice President, Finance Terri Lombardi
Vice President, Marketing Jeremy Biloon
Executive Director, Marketing Services Carol Pittard
Director, Brand Marketing Jean Kennedy
Finance Director Kevin Harrington
Sales Director Christi Crowley
Assistant General Counsel Andrew Goldberg
Assistant Director, Production Susan Chodakiewicz
Senior Manager, Category Marketing Bryan Christian
Brand Manager Katherine Barnet
Prepress Manager Alex Voznesenskiy
Project Manager Hillary Leary

Editorial Director Kostya Kennedy
Creative Director Gary Stewart
Director of Photography Christina Lieberman
Editorial Operations Director Jamie Roth Major
Senior Editor Alyssa Smith
Assistant Art Director Anne-Michelle Gallero
Copy Chief Rina Bander
Assistant Managing Editor Gina Scauzillo
Assistant Editor Courtney Mifsud

Special Thanks Don Armstrong, Melissa Frankenberry, Kristina Jutzi, Simon Keeble, Seniqua Koger, Kate Roncinske, Kristen Zwicker

Published by Time Books, an imprint of Time Inc. Books
225 Liberty Street · New York, NY 10281

We welcome your comments and suggestions about Time Books. Please write to us at: Time Books, Attention: Book Editors, P.O. Box 62310, Tampa, FL 33662-2310. If you would like to order any of our hardcover Collector's Edition books, please call us at 800-327-6388, Monday through Friday, 7 a.m.–9 p.m. Central Time.

Credits

FRONT AND BACK COVER
Peopleimages/Getty Images
TITLE PAGE
1 Ostill/iStock/Getty Images
CONTENTS
2 Tara Moore/Getty Images
INTRODUCTION
5 Matt Rainey/courtesy of Rodale Images **6** Courtesy Dr. Jordan D. Metzl
PART ONE
9 Tetra Images/Getty Images **10** Gjon Mili/The Life Picture Collection/Getty Images. Colorization by Sanna Dullaway **13** TIME **14–17** Gjon Mili/The Life Picture Collection/Getty Images; colorization by Sanna Dullaway (2) **19** iStock/Getty Images Plus **22–23** (chronological) Joe Vogan/Alamy Stock Photo; iStock/Getty Images Plus; Universal History Archive/Getty Images; DEA/G.Dagli Orti/Getty Images; Adoc-photos/Corbis/Getty Images; GraphicaArtis/Getty Images; Art Collection/Alamy stock photo; Popperfoto/Getty Images; courtesy of Museo Del Juego, The National Library of Medicine; Wikimedia Commons; Culture Club/Getty Images; Hulton Archive/Getty Images; Rembrandt Peale (oil on canvas from the White House collection, Washington, D.C.), 1853/photo by GraphicaArtis/Getty Images; Universal History Archive/UIG/Getty Images; The Granger Collection/Alamy stock photo; Ann Ronan Pictures/Print Collector/Getty Images; Ball State University, University Libraries. Archives and Special Collections; Louise Collection/Alamy stock photo; Topical Press Agency/Getty Images; George Rose/Getty Images; David Drew Zingg/Sports Illustrated; SilverScreen/Alamy stock photo; Steve Schapiro/Corbis/Getty Images; Emmanuel Dunand/AFP/Getty Images; Drew Angerer/Getty Images **25** Blend Images/Getty Images **26** Blend Images/Getty Images **28** Clive Brunskill/Getty Images **30** Al Bello/Getty Images **31** Eliot J. Schecter/NHLI/Getty Images **32** Andrew D. Bernstein/NBAE/Getty Images **34** Ezra Shaw/Getty Images **35** Clive Brunskill/Getty Images for The Laver Cup **36–37** iStock Photo/Getty Images
PART TWO
38 Nicole Hill/Rubberball/Getty Images **41** Ilbusca/Getty Images **42–43** Thomas Barwick/Getty Images **43** From top: Maskot/Getty Images; Maria Fuchs/Cultura/Getty Images; Bluecinema/Getty Images **44** Wetcake/DigitalVision Vectors/Getty Images **46** Robert Beck/Sports Illustrated **48** Marla Brose/Albuquerque Journal/ZUMA Wire/Alamy Live News **51** Tara Moore/Getty Images **52** Thomas Barwick/Getty Images **55** iStock/Getty Images Plus **56** Garo/Getty Images **58** From top: iStock/Getty Images; Science Source/Getty Images; iStock/Getty Images Plus; Martin Bureau/AFP/Getty Images **60** Aaron Kirking/courtesy of The Aviary **63** Paula Lobo/courtesy of The Metropolitan Museum of Art, New York **64** Robin Cerutti/courtesy of Aquastudio **67** Photo by Stefania Curto/courtesy of TrampoLEAN NYC **68–69** Venimo/iStock/Getty Images
PART THREE
71 iStock/Getty Images **73** Edwin Jimenez/Getty Images **74–75** From left: Seb Oliver/Getty Images; Hero Images/Getty Images; courtesy of Fitbit **76** Klaus Vedfelt/Getty Images **79** Andrew Paterson/Getty Images **80** iStock/Getty Images **83** Courtesy of McMaster University **84** Image Source/Getty Images **87** Courtesy Bryan Reece **88–89** Tom Pennington/Getty Images for Ironman (2) **90** Nigel Roddis/Getty Images for Ironman **92–93** iStock/Getty Images **94** Illustrations by Todd Detwiler for TIME **96** Neustockimages/Getty Images

FITNESS FACTS, TIPS AND MORE
HEAL YOURSELF
Right now, exercise is the best-known way to prevent Alzheimer's disease. On p. 24, find out what other magic it can work.
LEARN FROM TOP ATHLETES
Brain games, Pilates and meditation are the secrets to this pro 38-year-old volleyball player's success, on p. 28.
THE HISTORY OF EXERCISE
In 1772, sawing wood for a half hour each day was said to have almost cured a heart patient. Read about 24 other exercise milestones, on p. 22.
FIND YOUR BEST WORKOUT
Zumba started by accident. Now it's one of the best kinds of exercise for people who hate to work out. Find out why on p. 46.
WEIRD WAYS TO GET FIT
Ever wanted to dance through an art museum before it opens? Now you can. Three other unusual workouts, on p. 60.
MANAGING PAIN
There's a right and a wrong way to use ice for muscle soreness. The right way, on p. 54.
FINDING MOTIVATION
The hardest part of exercise is getting yourself to do it. Find 7 easy ways to get motivated, on p. 72.
FAST FITNESS
An intense workout you can do in just one minute, on p. 82.

Made in the USA
Monee, IL
12 August 2020

38325110R00059